D1568100

Living with Your Exchange Student

Ina Cherington

iUniverse, Inc.
Bloomington

iUniverse books may be ordered through booksellers or by contacting:

iUniverse
1663 Liberty Drive
Bloomington, IN 47403
www.iuniverse.com
1-800-Authors (1-800-288-4677)

ISBN: 978-1-4502-7619-1 (sc)
ISBN: 978-1-4502-7618-4 (ebook)

Printed in the United States of America

iUniverse rev. date: 01/14/2011

For my grandchildren
Sarah, Adam, Lindsey, Benjamin, Leah, and Shayna

Contents

Illustrations

Introduction: The Seed

Have you ever wondered why nearly half of the Vietnamese population has the surname Nguyen; what is served at a Japanese *kaiseki* dinner; and what *capoeira* means to Brazilians? These questions and countless others were answered during my twenty-one years as a regional manager and area representative (AR) for two different accredited high school exchange programs. My region included Denver and the north-central portion of Colorado known as the Front Range.

As manager, I wore many hats, often several at a time. My responsibilities included hiring, training, and supervising area representatives. The area representative's job is to place students with host families, interview the families in their home, check references, get school acceptance, and provide supervision and orientations.

I worked with schools to assure permission to enroll exchange students and oversaw an average of fifty students annually. Planning several activities throughout the year involved interacting with foreign students, their host families, the schools, and area representatives. Some days I required the skills of a psychologist, salesperson, or mediator, while at other times I was a counselor and social director. The position presented interesting challenges and required dynamic intervention and creative solutions.

My experiences, along with the knowledge I gained, led me down a lifelong cultural path. Receiving students from thirty countries, and traveling to the same number,—opened my eyes to the value of diversity. My desire to share those experiences and transport the reader into the world of cultural exchange prompted me to write *Living with Your Exchange Student*. Learning about cultural differences through international exchange leads to greater understanding and opens doors for world peace, one family at a time.

I will explore some of the many aspects of a high school exchange program: the host family, the exchange student, the area representative, the school, and the exchange organization. A chapter will be devoted to each component. One chapter describes travel opportunities for ARs, and another chronicles events in an exchange student calendar year. The final chapter explains cultural differences in language, customs, names, religion, and values. You will learn how Italians greet one another, which Brazilian city imported more African slaves than all of North America, and the differences in schools in other countries.

Long before becoming involved with foreign exchange students, my educational background was in horticulture. The biggest chunk of my adult work experience was as a landscape designer. When I began writing this book, the parallels between my two lines of work became apparent. I will describe the many similarities, and every chapter will be introduced with a brief comparison between trees and cultural exchange.

The story will resonate with current or past host families, pique the interest of—and provide important information for—those who are considering this valuable experience, and appeal to people intrigued by cultural diversity. *Living with Your Exchange Student* is a reflection on my adventures with exchange students, host families, and schools.

All the stories in this book are based on real incidents; the names of the people involved have been changed, however, to protect their privacy.

Chapter 1

The Newly Arriving Student—A Sapling

A newly arriving exchange student is like a sapling. Young, fragile, recently planted trees require certain essentials for survival, such as food, water, sunshine, and nutrients. Strong winds can uproot the delicate twig if not staked or supported. Some seedlings are hardy enough to survive despite neglect, but most require care. If planted properly in fertile soil, the roots will spread freely and corresponding branches will develop. There is work involved in growing a young tree to maturity, but the satisfaction and pleasure derived will exceed one's efforts. If the tree is nurtured and loved, it will produce shade, beauty, and possibly fruit for years to come, giving back far more than it received.

When exchange students arrive at the airport, exhausted from their long journey, they are nervous and vulnerable, despite being excited. They need nourishment, rest, and support. Of course, the host family provides the required room and board, but for the student to become an integrated family member and have a positive experience requires more than a bed and sustenance. If host parents provide guidance, warmth, and acceptance, chances for success are greater, and students begin to achieve their goals.

Some students have qualities that spell success in spite of challenges. Nevertheless, when a student steps out of everything that is familiar and is transplanted into a new environment, she may experience culture shock—a normal, temporary phenomenon. Whether it is transplant shock for a tree or culture shock for the exchange student, both need time to acclimate to their new locales. In a friendly atmosphere, the transition period shrinks, and adaptation occurs faster. If the hosts are overprotective or inflexible, the effect on the student is stifling. It is necessary for exchange students to extend their experiences beyond the host family.

Prior to leaving their home country, students attend an orientation. Exchange participants have another required briefing shortly after arriving in the United States. Host families also receive an orientation, conducted by their area representative, before their student arrives. In addition to the support provided to the student by the host family, the area representative who makes the placement acts as a liaison between the two, offering an ear when needed. She maintains contact and provides supervision throughout the home stay.

With love and care, trees will flourish, and exchange students will blossom. Hosting an exchange student is challenging and rewarding. Many host families comment that they get more from the exchange experience than they give. They now have a new family member, in addition to an understanding of a foreign culture.

Chapter 2

Host Family—The Roots

Just as roots are what anchor a tree, the host family provides the foundation for the exchange student and her American[1] experience. Without a firm base, neither the tree nor the student is well grounded. Vital to the tree's health are its roots. Strong roots are essential, but when you purchase a tree, the roots aren't visible. Based on other factors, such as leaves, branches, and trunk, you hope to determine that the tree is healthy. Similarly, an in-home interview is required in order to evaluate the suitability of a potential host family. Asking the right questions, having them complete an application, checking references, performing a background check, and a gut feeling that comes from years of experience may make the selection process easier. Identifying a family's motivation for hosting is part of the in-home interview. Providing a safe environment for students is essential.

Hosting a foreign exchange student is an exciting but demanding responsibility, not to be taken lightly, but rather with thoughtful consideration. It should be a family decision. Those who take this leap of faith will have a gratifying, educational experience.

So who wants to parent someone else's teenager for five or ten months? All sorts of people choose to host. They are nurses, teachers, bus drivers, artists, attorneys,

---

1. All references to "American" or "America" refer to the United States.

physicians, plumbers, engineers, architects, store owners, pilots, retirees, military personnel, restaurant owners, police officers, former Peace Corps volunteers, landscapers, farmers, ministers, CEOs, software developers and information technology people, stay-at-home mothers, stay-at-home-fathers, politicians, psychologists, social workers, car salesmen—even the governor of Colorado, prior to being elected.

By no means are families always traditional, with two parents and two children. Many families—but not all—have teenagers. Sometimes hosts are single parents, single people, empty nesters, young couples without children, and families with young children. Families with only children have the space and often host.

One family hosted for eight straight years, taking a student from a different country every time. Another family, with seven children of their own, claimed there was always room for another child. Dozens of families in my area have hosted several times. The Department of State permits double placements as long as the two students don't speak the same language. Parents of both exchange students have to agree, as does the host family and the school.

Double placements are infrequent but there are some. When I was training a new representative and she was feeling unsure about making her first placement, I would offer to go to the family interview. At one such meeting, the husband and wife could not agree whether to host a boy or a girl. The wife wanted a girl and the husband a boy, and neither would budge. Finally, they asked if they could host both. They were empty nesters and thought that two students would be company for one another.

They successfully hosted a girl from Germany and a boy from Mexico and went on to host other students, one at a time. After years of hosting, the mom became an area representative.

Why would a family consider hosting an exchange student? Different motivations prompt people to host, but monetary gain is not one of them, since the families are not financially compensated. One of the main reasons given for hosting is to provide a high school student the opportunity to experience American culture while the host family learns about another country. Some families hope to visit their student's country and have a personal contact or learn something about their heritage. Others express how fortunate their own lives have been and they want the opportunity to give back by welcoming a young person into their home. Families with strong religious beliefs are frequent hosts. Above all, the host family wants an enjoyable experience for all concerned. Communicative families—as well as stable, flexible ones—are the most successful.

The most frequently asked question is, "What if it doesn't work?" Families and students need the assurance that when all efforts to work things out fail, the student will be moved to a new family. The majority of problems stem from lack of communication.

Occasionally, only children have a difficult time sharing their parents. Some parents handle the situation well; others don't. An example of a hosting situation that worked especially well was a family with an only teenage daughter, Diane. When Irina arrived from Croatia, the two girls appeared to have little in common. Diane had just entered adolescence and lacked confidence. She resented Irina, who was older—more mature and self-assured. Diane had never shared her parents with anyone and resented the attention that Irina received. Sensitive to the problem, the wise host mom assembled a large bag of nice used clothing. Understanding the universal interest in fashion among teenage girls, she hoped for a connection. The two girls went through the pile, laughing as they tried on the clothes and hats, deciding what they would keep and what to donate to less fortunate teens. After sharing this experience, Diane gradually became more tolerant of Irina. By the end of the year, they had bonded. Both girls married, and they attended each other's weddings. Irina, an architect, has two children. She lived in Paris for a while and then moved to Prague with her husband and sons. Diane, a teacher, married several years later and continues to live in Colorado. Some twenty years later Diane and Irina remain friends, managing to see each other every three or four years.

In another instance, a single mom and her ten-year-old daughter lived in a beautiful home and were initially excited about hosting. It was not obvious at the interview, or from references, that this attractive, young mother spent little time at home. Her motivation was to have a companion for her daughter. The family selected Kristen, a German girl. She and her host mom got along well, but the daughter didn't want to share her mother. Since the young girl spent so little time with her mother, she viewed Kristen as bothersome competition for the attention she craved.

It became apparent within the first month that hosting an exchange student was a mistake for this pair. Fortunately, the area representative was able to place

Kristen with a caring, traditional family that provided her with a positive experience for the remainder of the school year. The new family had been one of the references for the single mom. When the area representative began searching for a replacement for Kristen, he contacted one of the references, and they decided to host.

Prospective hosts sometimes ask if there is any country whose students cause more difficulty than another. They want to know if girls are easier than boys or the other way around. I can honestly respond that no one nationality presents more problems. Neither gender is easier. Over time, I observed cultural similarities within a country, although generalizations can't be applied to individuals. For example, Vietnamese are serious students, Brazilians are the most social, and Germans speak the best English because they begin studying it in school at an early age.

Many hosts live in small houses, others in mansions. Some of the best placements are in modest homes. Throughout the United States, placements in large cities are rare. Most families live in the suburbs or in small towns. In Colorado, students sometimes have placements on farms and ranches with horses, while others are in mountain communities.

Marina, a Brazilian girl from São Paulo, a city of seventeen million people, was having a particularly difficult adjustment to a small mountain town. Houses are far apart, and sometimes the closest neighbor is separated by acres. Students from large cities are used to walking or using public transportation to get where they want to go. In the mountains, a car is necessary. Marina's host parents worked. When the bus brought her home from school, she had nowhere to go. She grumbled, "The only thing I can do is talk to the squirrels." After that, I tried to be more attuned to which students would do well in isolated areas. Most students accept placements anywhere in the United States; for an additional fee they can request a particular area. The Northeast, Florida, and California are popular choices.

Although students can share a bedroom, if they have their own beds, placements where they have their own space work best. Basement rooms are acceptable as long as there is an egress window or proximity to the stairs for easy access. Exchange students have their own health insurance and spending money.

When a family makes the decision to host an exchange student, it is prudent to identify one of the programs listed with the Council on Standards for International Educational Travel (CSIET), the agency that evaluates exchange programs. Local schools are a good source for recommending programs that send students who possess the qualities that enable them to succeed. Adequate language skills, maturity, teacher recommendations, and solid academic records contribute to successful placements. CSIET prints a list of the approved programs online. According to CSIET, twenty-nine thousand foreign high school students came to the United States in 2007–2008. The number of students and the number of agencies handling them have increased in recent years.

CSIET suggests that American schools should ideally work toward accepting exchange students to make up 1 percent of the student population. The US Department of State claims that secondary school student exchange programs have been part of US public diplomacy efforts since 1949. These programs promote mutual understanding by providing foreign students the opportunity to study in American high schools while living with an American host family. Not only are the students themselves transformed by these experiences, so too are their families, friends, and teachers back home. Americans, such as the host families, students, and sponsor representatives whose lives intersect with these students, benefit as well.

Sometimes, when there are unusual circumstances, the interview is challenging for the AR. One summer, on a Sunday afternoon, I drove to a prospective family home for an interview. After parking my car, I approached a modest bungalow with an attractive front yard. I rang the doorbell and, while waiting, admired the effective use of succulents, surrounded by rocks, and the absence of lawn—a xeriscape. The potential host mom welcomed me, but I was not prepared for what greeted me inside. Kate, a nurse, with whom I had spoken on the phone several times, had told me that her son Brian had cerebral palsy; I hadn't comprehended, however, to what extent.

Brian, a severely handicapped, wheelchair-bound boy, had no verbal skills. His handsome face wore a pleasant expression, and he smiled freely when I was introduced to him and Jim, his father. Brian, who was eleven at the time, enjoyed stimulation and having people around. He was able to communicate with a voice computer.

Complicating matters further, Jim had neuro-fibromatosis. According to the National Institute of Neurological Disorders and Stroke this disease is a genetic neurological disorder, causing tumors to grow on nerves and produce abnormalities such as skin changes and bone deformities. In Jim's case, he had large skin lesions on his face. I had never seen anyone afflicted with this disease.

Jim was a stay-at-home dad who volunteered at Brian's school.

My initial discomfort almost prevented me from placing a student with this caring couple. I tried not to stare at Brian or Jim for too long, but I didn't want to appear rude by not looking at them. I was grateful that the application provided a focus. As the interview with the parents progressed, I questioned whether I could find a student who would feel at ease in this situation. I reminded myself that exchange programs show no discrimination against disabled exchange students or families with disabilities.

The remarkably calm parents were so at ease with each other, and so relaxed in their handling of Brian, that, after a while, I started to feel more comfortable. Together, we filled out the application. I then took the customary tour of the house. When I got home, I called their references. All of them were good. With some reservations on my part, I placed a boy from Vietnam who indicated that he had worked with handicapped children. Of course, the family medical history was revealed to Minh and his natural parents. As soon as Minh enthusiastically accepted the placement, my concerns diminished. That began my long relationship with Kate and Jim. I later learned that Brian had been the local cerebral palsy poster child.

Before the year was half over, an Ecuadorian friend and classmate of Minh's was looking for a new host family. Brian's parents immediately offered to host him too. There was no end to the generosity and acceptance of this couple. They loved young people. Since that year, they have hosted a total of six students. Next to the American flag that always hung on their front porch was the flag from their current exchange student's country. The last time I passed the house, there were three red, white, and blue flags. In addition to the United States, Thailand and the Czech Republic were represented. The red and white flag of Poland was also displayed. Every one of Kate and Jim's exchange students has come back to visit, a few during the summer, others for extended periods. To my knowledge, some are still here attending college.

Hosts range in age from midtwenties to midseventies, with most hosts between thirty and fifty. In some cases, the children are grown, and the couple is helping to raise a grandchild.

The Nelsons, now grandparents, are an example. When their son was in high school, they hosted Adem from Germany, who is of Turkish descent. With his thick head of wavy, black hair, dark skin, and tall, lean build, he looked Middle Eastern. Although he was born in Germany, he identified with his Turkish culture. He was a talented dancer, with a style adapted from break dancing. During the annual fall retreat in the mountains, Adem provided unplanned entertainment. Supporting himself on one hand, then the other, without losing momentum, he spun like a whirling dervish, with the dexterity of a juggler, mesmerizing the entire group. Years later, Adem returned for his host brother's wedding. He continues to have contact with his host family.

The Nelsons and I kept in touch with yearly Christmas cards. After seven years, when they were empty-nester grandparents, I received a call that they had decided to host again. Mr. Nelson had suffered a mild stroke and was no longer working, but still driving and active. Rita asked me to select a student for them. Since I didn't want them to compare another student to Adem, I selected a girl from a different part of the world.

Yuki, a petite Japanese girl with a smiling, round, moon face, charmed them. Academically, she ranked No. 1 out of a class of 575 students, as well as lettering in swimming and lacrosse. She assisted in the advanced Japanese class. The Nelsons surprised Yuki with a trip to Florida when she finished school, before she returned to Japan. They knew that she wanted to go to Disney World. When they returned, I asked Yuki what she enjoyed the most. Without a second's hesitation, she responded, "The alligators." Disney World was a close second.

Sometimes families want to host but don't want to commit to a semester or a year. For people like them, many exchange organizations offer Independent Home Stays lasting from two to four weeks, in addition to the full, academic-year program. Many short-term hosts have a positive experience and later on have a full-year student in their home.

Reina and Naoki's sons had both been high school exchange students. Some years later, the sons' positive experiences inspired their parents to come to the United States on a short-term program. They thought that spending three weeks with a family would give them a taste of the United States. They requested Colorado, and I placed them with a family that had hosted a German girl a few years earlier.

A couple of weeks before the Japanese couple was to arrive, the host family with whom I had matched them realized that it was their college freshman daughter's parents' weekend. They had been busy getting their daughter ready for college and hadn't noticed at the time of the placement that there was a conflict. Of course, they wanted to attend parents' weekend. Since it was late to find another family, we invited Reina and Naoki to stay at our house for five days.

When I greeted them at the airport, I realized that Reina, a frail, diminutive woman, spoke little English and Naoki, a sturdy, taller-than-average Japanese man, even less. Several years earlier, I had visited Japan and learned a few phrases that I remembered. My limited knowledge of Japanese consisted of the greetings *hajimemash'te, ohayo,* and *sayonara.* After I had asked them how they were and said "good morning" and "good-bye," the conversation ended. Reina's English was significantly better than my Japanese. Writing helped. English classes in Japan emphasize writing and reading, not speaking. Communicating nonverbally is challenging and fun but has its limitations.

While I was in the kitchen, simmering a stew on the stove and making a salad for the first evening's dinner, Reina quietly appeared from the downstairs guest bedroom and handed me a piece of paper. She had written the question, "Do you have any rice?" Whisking the 1983 Uncle Ben's forty-year anniversary, orange canister out of the cupboard, I removed the lid, which sported a picture of smiling Uncle Ben. Proudly, I showed her the ample supply. She squinted as she suspiciously eyed the rice and reached into the tin, picking up a small handful. She briefly rubbed a few kernels back and forth between her thumb and index finger before opening her palm, spreading her fingers apart, and casting the alien grains back into the container, confirming what I had guessed. This wasn't sticky rice, which is what she had in mind.

Following dinner the first evening, we watched and listened to a video. Reina's hobby was photography, and prior to her arrival she had prepared a two-hour film of gardens and places of interest in Japan. We saw images of cherry trees blossoming, Japanese gardens, Japanese red maples, close-ups of single flowers, and shots of the city where Reina and Naoki lived. The video was beautiful but long. Phil, my partner in cultural exchange, as well as my mate in all life's experiences, kept falling asleep. I continued elbowing him, at which time he would wake up with a start and snort. In a few minutes his head would fall back, and again he'd be asleep. Though I was fearful of offending our guests, I didn't need to worry because they were so polite that, if they noticed, they pretended they didn't. Nobody laughed. After we watched the video, Reina and Naoki presented it to us with several other gifts, each beautifully wrapped, in appreciation for our hospitality.

The next day we visited the botanical gardens. It was an Indian summer morning, with many plants still in bloom and few people enjoying them. Fall is an excellent time for such an outing because the summer crowds are gone, and it isn't beastly hot. We leisurely strolled the garden paths for close to two hours before going into the conservatory. I am sure it only seemed like Reina photographed every flower, but if she didn't, she didn't miss too many. I couldn't tell whether or not she and Naoki liked the Japanese garden; it was the only area she did not photograph, probably because there are so many beautiful gardens in Japan.

After touring the gardens, we drove to Sakura Square, a small plaza in lower downtown Denver, where there are restaurants, a series of stores selling Asian products, and a large Japanese market. Following lunch, Reina and Naoki wanted to go to the market. As soon as we entered the store, Naoki started piling items into a shopping cart from the aisles of fresh vegetables, packaged goods, frozen items, and canned goods. Daikon, taro root, burdock, and *gaighoi*, were names of vegetables I remembered from Japanese menus but had never seen before. Several shelves displayed household and decorative items, such as teapots, bowls, and dishes. Naoki bought half a dozen containers of sticky rice in white Styrofoam cartons with Japanese writing on clear, plastic lids. Reina approved. A prepared golden curry sauce in a colorful carton was the next item in the basket. When they were satisfied with their purchases, we waited in a short checkout line. Naoki insisted upon paying for everything.

Saturday morning Naoki cooked breakfast for everyone. I can still picture the eggs, sitting next to the pan-fried salmon, with a tomato garnish that came from my garden. After breakfast, Naoki started the preparation for an authentic Japanese dinner with the ingredients that he had bought at the market the previous day. The meal was delicious and beautifully presented, complemented by good china and silver. Eating in the dining room provided a festive atmosphere. Reina took many photos before we ate.

Our visit was progressing nicely, although it had only been three days. Finding someone who spoke Japanese seemed like a brilliant idea, and that's when I called the Dawsons and explained the situation. They were hosting a third Japanese girl and came to my aid. Their motivation for hosting was that their only daughter, Carol, had become interested in Japanese culture and language. She had studied Japanese for several years in high school and had become quite proficient. Shortly after finishing high school, Carol visited Japan and stayed with the families of the girls they had hosted. Natural parents enjoy reciprocating. It is not always possible, but many people visit their exchange students in their home countries. The generous hospitality extended to host family members is memorable.

The Dawsons and their Japanese exchange student offered to take Reina and Naoki to the mountains on Sunday. Carol's grandfather joined them. They went fishing, one of Naoki's favorite activities. He caught several good-sized rainbow trout. Reina photographed the fish, the lake, the mountains, and their hosts. Everyone had an exhilarating day, and Carol was happy to practice her Japanese. Later that evening we met them for dinner at The Fort, a well-known Denver restaurant in the foothills, recognized for serving buffalo. It was a congenial, lively group whose members felt comfortable with one another. It had been a successful Sunday.

Two days later the Japanese couple joined the family that had agreed to host them for the remainder of their stay. I drove them ten miles to a large, stately home in one of Denver's older neighborhoods. Following introductions to their new hosts and a tour of the house, I made sure my new friends had collected their suitcases and belongings from my car. After hugging each other, Reina and I parted somewhat tearfully. Driving home alone, I marveled at how these lovely people had endeared themselves to me so profoundly in such a short time. I visited them again before they went back to Japan.

Several times a year, Reina e-mails pictures of her grandchildren, herself, Naoki, flowers, gardens, scenes of their city, and the German boy they hosted after their return. We have an open-ended invitation to visit them. The following year, Carol's family visited Reina and Naoki in Japan. I can only imagine the extent of the hospitality shown to them.

Another family, who had a disappointing first hosting experience, went on to have many successful ones. The Millers felt confident that they were a good host family, even though their first attempt, with a Mexican girl, wasn't successful. Rosa never bonded with the Millers. Sometimes personalities just don't mesh. Having a positive experience was important to them. They subsequently hosted girls from Brazil, Romania, and Mexico. A Spanish girl who was clashing with her host mother spent her free time at their house. All the girls still contact the family regularly. This family would have continued to host but they became involved with raising their grandson. The dad told me that hosting exchange students was among the most memorable and best experiences of his life.

Not all families have such a positive experience. An example of a problematic situation was with the family who hosted Jorge, from Spain. The family found fault with him the entire time. It was never anything serious, just nitpicking details. His sister had been with a different family the previous year. She started out quite reserved and truly blossomed during her stay. I had hopes for Jorge, but according to his host mom he didn't appear interested in participating in family activities. His lack of initiative in making friends disturbed her.

The AR suggested that she find another home for him. It seemed like it might be a relief for everyone, although Jorge never complained. The family had made a commitment for an entire school year, and they were determined to honor that commitment. A year later, I found out that the hosts had traveled to Spain during the summer to visit Jorge and his family and had an absolutely wonderful time. They appreciated him much more in his familiar family surroundings and with his friends.

There were similar situations where friendships continued after the exchange student went home, in spite of the fact that the families didn't seem to get the most from the experience while the student was here. At other times, students who didn't appear to enjoy their stay continued to call and e-mail their host family when they returned to their native country. Incompatibility with a sibling can cause friction even though the student gets along well with the rest of the family. Sometimes admiration for one another takes time to develop, and the full benefits are realized only after the student leaves.

I would be remiss to close the chapter about host families without mentioning pets. According to an article in *Business Week* on August 6, 2007, forty-one billion dollars was spent on pets in the United States that year. It is not surprising that almost every host family has one or more domestic animals. This same affection is not shared in many other countries and cultures. Islamic countries consider the saliva from dogs unclean; therefore dogs are not permitted inside the house. In rural areas of Korea and China, dogs are used for human consumption. In large cities, such as São Paulo, Mexico City, and Tokyo, people live in apartments or flats and don't have room for pets.

Some of my favorite stories involve pets, but not necessarily the furry kind. If students indicated that they were allergic, or simply didn't want a placement in a home with animals, they had more difficulty getting a placement. The student application indicates whether they can adjust to pets or prefer a home without animals. Whenever I spoke to potential hosts on the telephone prior to the home interview, one of the questions I would ask was, "Do you have any pets?"

During the telephone interview with the Clarks, I forgot to ask this important question. Later, I arrived at their house with several bios, but I had a Brazilian girl in mind for this family. The home interview confirmed my thoughts—that Inga would be a good match. She liked young children, and this family had three. She was willing to attend church, which was important to the parents. Interests were similar. The Clarks read several bios and selected Inga. She was the ideal fit, except for one problem. Inga was afraid of pets and indicated on her application that she didn't want a home with animals.

About the time I asked about pets, the family's Bouvier des Flandres, who had been sequestered in the kitchen, was released, and he galloped into the living room like a small pony. This giant breed is an impressive, powerfully built dog. It gained a reputation for herding cattle and pulling carts. Beau ran over to where I was seated and started to sniff where all dogs sniff. He then planted his massive, black head, with beard, mustache, and shaggy eyebrows, in my lap. Shortly, with some prompting from the dad, Beau lay down on his back with his legs extended in the air. His paws approached the height of the arm of my chair. The family quickly assured me that dogs of this breed look intimidating but are gentle and make good pets. It didn't take much to convince me. Persuaded by the family and by Beau's pleasant, calm nature, I proceeded with the interview.

In a short while, I took the customary tour of the house to see the prospective student's bedroom and bathroom. Suddenly, a twenty-pound cat, looking more like a puma than a domestic shorthair, leaped in front of me and darted into one of the bedrooms. This giant, gray feline named George was anything but calm. What to do? Not one, but two, of the largest animals of their breed were revered family members. Sharing my concern with the parents didn't change anything. The children jumped up and down screaming, "We want Inga," having already seen her photo. They had made their selection. I suggested that we put the placement through and ask Inga if she would accept a family with pets. The Clarks agreed, and Inga accepted.

Several months later, shortly before school started, Inga arrived and made a smooth transition. She adjusted to the family and even became attached to the pets. Her host family loved her. Inga's Brazilian family lived in an apartment, so she had never had pets. Because of lack of exposure, Inga thought she was afraid.

Following her high school year, she returned to Brazil, but she came back to the United States to attend college, again living with her host family. Inga's biological mother had died when Inga was young, and her father had remarried. Since she had bonded with her host family, including Beau and George, and the feeling was mutual, the Clarks eventually legally adopted her. Inga is now living in Brazil with her husband and two children. She and her host family stay in touch, and they visit her. After this experience, I didn't concern myself as much with pet fears—only pet allergies.

My favorite pet story involved a professional couple and their two young sons. They lived in an old Victorian house within the city limits. They had hosted several times before taking a break. It had been a year or so since I had visited the Spencers. The Department of State requires a home visit every time a family wishes to host because something could have changed. When I asked if anything had changed since I was there last, Susan said, "You haven't met Winston Churchill." I replied, "You're right," not yet knowing Winston's identity, but assuming he had four legs.

After completing the application, I followed Susan downstairs to see the student's room in the finished basement. Until then, they had hosted boys, but they had decided to host a girl this time. She would have her own room and bath, which I had seen before.

Then I met Winston Churchill, who, from the tip of his nose to the end of his scaly tail was a six-foot-long, pale-green iguana with substantial claws. He looked like a cross between a prehistoric creature and a mythical dragon. The fold that hung from his neck, called a dewlap, gave new meaning to an enlarged Adam's apple. Winston Churchill was housed in a glass cage that covered an entire wall, directly across from the student's room. The cage had been built especially for him. At a quick glance, because of the clear glass, it appeared that nothing separated Winston from the viewer. In order to get from the bedroom to the bathroom, it was necessary to pass the cage. The first thing their student would see every morning, before she brushed her teeth, was Winston Churchill.

Susan Spencer, an architect with a bubbly personality, was a volunteer at the zoo. She explained that it was not unusual for people to buy small exotic pets, and when they became unmanageable, they would bring them to the zoo. Several weeks had passed since this large iguana had been brought to the zoo, and no one had adopted him. His future wasn't looking promising until Susan rescued him.

Months passed and Maria, the Spencers' Ecuadorian student, adjusted surprisingly well to her floor mate. One day, when I made my routine bimonthly call to check on Maria's progress, the host dad reported that everything was fine with Maria, but that they had had some excitement and theatrics. Since my last call, they had hired a new cleaning woman. Forgetting to tell Stella about Winston Churchill proved a major mistake. Her first day on the job, she went downstairs to vacuum, saw the beast, screamed, and promptly fainted. By the time the paramedics arrived, Stella had revived.

After that incident, I made sure that family photo albums included pictures of all family members, including pets. In the past, the photos were mailed to the exchange students family. Now family and pet pictures are available online with the complete host family application.

You have now read about many different host families, as well as their pets, that have created lifelong bonds of friendship with their exchange students. These lasting emotional ties contribute to international understanding. In many cases, the exchange student and host family become intertwined like the roots of a tree—impossible to separate.

Chapter 3

Exchange Students—What Variety!

Students come from thirty countries, on three continents, offering countless cultural differences. Similarly, one has a vast selection to choose from when planting a tree. One might want a tree that provides shade, an ornamental that produces spring blossoms, a fruit tree that supplies food, or a fir that displays year-round greenery.

Some families request a student from France, Italy, or Spain, while others prefer one from Japan, China, or Vietnam. If a family lived in Germany and had a wonderful experience, they sometimes want to host a German student to return the hospitality that was lavished upon them. On the other hand, families often want to learn more about their own heritage and request a student who comes from the same country as their grandparents. A Spanish speaker may be of interest if a family's children are studying the language. Many families don't care which country the student is from and are more concerned about compatibility. If they are an active family interested in hiking, skiing, and other outdoor activities, a student whose main interests are reading, computers, and movies isn't the best match and will be happier with a family who enjoys spending time as she does. Sometimes parents hope for a friend for their shy teenager. It is important to remember, however, that students are not nannies and to make sure the family isn't looking for an au pair; some students, on the other hand, enjoy young children and request such a placement.

Exchange students are between fifteen and eighteen and a half and are carefully screened in their home countries by partner organizations. Every applicant undergoes a comprehensive interview process to determine maturity, motivation, and spoken English ability. Applicants are required to have adequate language proficiency, enabling them to take their classes in English. Two teacher recommendations are required, and one is usually from an English teacher. Students are expected to write a letter in English without the help of a teacher or parent. Part of the application includes three years of transcripts.

A physical exam is necessary, although most disabilities don't prevent students from being accepted. The student must be current on all inoculations or receive those shots prior to being admitted to the American school. All exchange students are required to have health insurance. The policies also cover dental and theft. Pre-existing conditions are not covered. When everything is completed, the full application is sent to the American partner. The sponsoring organization decides whether or not it wants to accept the student. Once accepted, the applicant must be placed with a family by August 31.

Completing the comprehensive, twenty-page student application can take weeks. It requires time to schedule a doctor's appointment, get the teacher recommendations, provide photos, and for the exchange student to write a letter that will be read by potential host families. Just as the American family sends pictures, so does the exchange student. The American family can view photos of the exchange student's home and family, and the exchange student's family can see where their son or daughter will be living and with whom.

The program I worked with accepted about one thousand students a year, with an equal number of girls and boys. Colorado, however, always places more girls than boys. It seems that if families have daughters, they want girls, and if they have sons, they think it might be fun to have a daughter. Placements in the Front Range have to be made early because of school deadlines, and girls are still available. Frequently only boys are available by July.

Determining the right student for a family is like being a matchmaker. One can look at similar interests, religion, family structure, academics, and what the parents do for a living. It isn't known, however, whether the personalities will blend. Finding out as much information as possible about the family beforehand helps. In some cases, a family would select a student other than the one I thought was the best fit. I would offer guidance, but the final decision belonged to the family. I would ask each family member to rank their choices one, two, and three. In some cases, everyone in the family would rank them differently. Then the family would take the night to think about it and make a decision, usually by the next day. If they waited too long, the student they wanted might have been placed elsewhere. After a family selects a student and before they arrive, there is ample opportunity to e-mail one another and become acquainted.

Two weeks before students arrived in August, an orientation and international potluck were held in my backyard for the host families of the students Phil and I were supervising. It was usually on a weekday evening.

Combining the orientation with dinner gave the families a chance to get to know one another. After the families had a chance to meet, eat, and socialize, I would conduct the orientation. Generally, between twelve and fifteen families attended. Teenage host brothers and sisters were encouraged to come, although I discouraged bringing young children because they get bored and are a distraction for their parents. During the meeting, which lasted several hours, I answered questions, did some role-playing, and thanked the families for their participation.

Some people were nervous about what they had committed to, and it was always comforting to the "new parents" when repeat families spoke up and talked about how they had handled problems in previous years. As former hosts, their suggestions were credible. Typically during this meeting, I presented sensible goals, and expectations were set, as well as practical information given. I also explained airport pickup procedure, what to do if luggage was lost, what happened if the student missed her plane, etc.

In order to help families to have realistic expectations, I always passed on a quote that seemed appropriate: "Exchange students descend from airplanes, not from heaven." Parents shouldn't show partiality to the exchange student, or their own son or daughter will pick it up in a heartbeat and resent the new arrival. On the other hand, it is unfair to give privileges to family teenagers that are not granted to the exchange student. It is the exchange student who makes the most adjustments. I would encourage host families not to change their lifestyle, or they would resent their visitor. The idea is to help this young person adapt to everything new and different and become a family member. They are here too long to be a guest in the house.

I encouraged families to plan minimal activities for the first few days after the student's arrival. Students need time to get over jet lag, rest, and begin the adjustment process. I suggest that, following a tour of the house, the student be given a tour of the neighborhood and the school she will be attending. Taking the student to a supermarket and allowing her to buy necessary toiletry items or something she likes to eat for breakfast is a good way to begin the first days. Showing the exchange student simple things like how to use appliances, which are probably different than the ones in their home country, is helpful. Registration for classes takes place shortly after arrival.

Parents need to tell their students what they want to be called; otherwise they will probably remain nameless. Exchange students want to know if they are to use "Mom" and "Dad" or first names. Since the words in the students' language are different, the teens don't mind using these endearing words. Some host siblings, however, don't want anyone else calling their parents Mom and Dad. Most parents ask to be called by their first name.

Another recommendation I have is to discuss and write down the family rules and expectations. Writing the information is critical, because students smile and act like they understand what you are saying, but frequently they get only partial meanings, especially in the beginning. Posting the list of rules in a prominent place avoids confusion because reading in a new language is easier than speaking or listening.

At first, I planned and scheduled events throughout the year without much notice. As the group grew, I realized that advance planning was more efficient. Compiling a schedule of the events and giving a copy to host families at the initial meeting improved attendance. They could mark important dates on their calendar and not plan other activities. The following is a sample schedule.

July 27 6:00–9:00 p.m.	Orientation for host families; International Potluck
	Bring a dish to share from your exchange student's country
Location: 1800 Main St., Denver, CO.	
August	Student arrivals the first two weeks of August
	Meet and Greet at airport
Sunday, August 29	Orientation for exchange students and families
	Required for exchange students
5:00–8:00 p.m.	Barbecue and swimming party at the Smith's home. Hamburgers, hot dogs, and beverages … will be provided. Bring a side dish to share.
September 12–14	Call students and families
September 26–28	Call students and families

October 9	Pumpkin Patch harvest at Chatfield Arboretum for the region
	Families are welcome to attend.
	Meet at 9:00 a.m. at the entrance. Wear comfortable clothing and close-toed shoes. Free tickets for the maze when harvesting is completed.
	All-you-can-eat buffet lunch at Country Buffet at noon. Cost $12.
	Arrange carpools.
October 24–26	Call students and families.
November 7–9	Call students and families.
November 15–17	Call students and families.
Sunday, December 5	Holiday/Christmas Party and Gift Exchange 4:00–6:00 p.m. at

Amy's, 3540 State St. The ARs will provide food and beverages. Bring a $10 wrapped gift, suitable for a boy or girl. Host siblings are invited to attend. For the region.

December 13–15	Call students and host families
January—first week	Second semester students arriving.
	Meet and Greet at airport
January 15–17	Call students and host families
January 22 3:00 p.m.	Orientation for second semester students. Required.
4:00 p.m. –6:00 p.m.	Required midyear orientation for AYP students
	Location to be announced
	Exchange students bring a dish to share from your home country.
February 13–15	Call students and host families
February 25–27	Call students and host families
March 15	Pizza Party at Beau Jo's for students and families

March 28–30	Call students and host families
April 5–7	Call students and host families
Sunday, April 18	Rockies baseball game. Students and families are invited. Tickets $12
May 12	Required reentry orientation. Students only. Location to be announced.

Sometimes changes became necessary. For instance, one year I inadvertently scheduled the midyear meeting at the same time as the Super Bowl. The exchange students didn't mind as much as the host parents, who let me know that they didn't want to carpool during the game.

In most cases, I joined the host family at the airport to meet and greet their student. It is recommended that ARs greet their student when they arrive. If this isn't possible, they are to meet them within forty-eight hours. It was fun to be a part of the excitement and anticipation the family was experiencing. After exchanging e-mails and photos for weeks or months, the student and family finally met. Armed with welcoming signs, balloons, sometimes flowers and cameras, families waited anxiously for their student to step off the escalator and into view.

Unfortunately, the days of meeting arrivals at the gate ended with 9/11. Since then, exchange students arriving at Denver International Airport (DIA) are advised to deplane, walk from the gate down the steps to the train, exit at the terminal, and ascend escalators to a crowd waiting behind a waist-high barrier. In waves, dozens of travelers step off the two escalators that are on opposite sides of the restricted area, separated by some thirty feet. Spotting the person you are waiting for is like watching a tennis match and trying to keep your eye on the ball. Years of experience taught me that if the student and family don't connect within twenty-five minutes, something is wrong. The student either missed her flight; the flight is later than the arrival board indicates; or, in a few cases, the student is being detained at the gate.

Occasionally, the natural parents pay an extra fee to have their unaccompanied minor escorted throughout her journey. In that case, the foreign student is held at the gate, under supervision by airline personnel. It is then necessary for a host family member to go to the airline ticket counter and get a pass to go down to the gate and have the student released to their host parent. The airlines will issue only one pass per family.

In a few situations, a student will come up the escalator, not see her family, and disappear, heading for baggage claim. Those are the times when the area representative is helpful. She can check at the baggage claim area while the family waits at the designated meeting spot.

Every so often the flight arrives on time, but the student has missed her connection. The students are advised to call their host families if that happens. The families then know to meet a later flight. It is wise to check arrival times before going to the airport. Families should allow enough time because sometimes a flight arrives earlier than expected. It doesn't make a good first impression if the student isn't welcomed properly.

If students arrive directly into DIA from their home country and have to go through customs, the meeting place and procedure are different. These passengers are met at the international gate. Because they have to go through customs before exiting through closed doors, people trickle out a few at a time, and it takes close to an hour, but they have their luggage with them.

The vast majority of students arrive without incident. A look of relief, evidenced by a smile, transforms their tired faces when they recognize their new family holding up a welcome sign with their name. After the family and students have a few minutes to hug or shake hands and properly greet one another, I introduce myself. While walking to the baggage claim area, I welcome the student, making sure that she knows I am her area representative. To access the student's level of English, one of my questions is, "What do you know about Denver?" Regardless of their nationality, most of the boys know about the Broncos. With Internet access, they have already checked out their high school. I always remind them to call their natural parents and let them know that they have arrived safely.

In the instances when luggage doesn't turn up, the host parents should file a claim before leaving the area. The missing baggage generally arrives on the next flight, and the airlines arrange to have it delivered to the house. As soon as I am sure that their luggage has arrived, I leave the student and family to begin their long-anticipated first day. The first weeks are generally the "honeymoon period." Questions arise, but host families and students are excited as they get to know one another.

The exchange students always come with presents for their host family. As their area representative, I too was the recipient of many gifts over the years. Our china cabinet is filled with curios from around the world. There are Japanese lacquered bowls, Chinese teapots, Brazilian rocks, a model of a Vietnamese rickshaw, a miniature Mongolian yurt, and a Danish flask. We have coffee table books from Germany, Macedonia, Croatia, and China. Handmade doilies, kitchen towels, and table linens represent three different continents. Of course, there are the edible gifts of chocolates from Germany, which are always appreciated.

The students arrive from Eastern and Western Europe, Latin America, and Asia. In the late eighties and early nineties, the majority of students were Spanish, but subsequently Germany became the biggest sending partner. The next largest group comes from Brazil. Every year there are Ecuadorians, Vietnamese, Hungarians, Japanese, Polish, South Koreans, and Thai. In recent years, we started receiving more students from France, Italy, Denmark, Sweden, Norway, Finland, and China.

We also receive students from the Ukraine, Armenia, Azerbaijan, Tajikistan, and several other Central Asian countries, thanks to the Future Leaders Exchange. It was started in 1992 when Senator Bill Bradley introduced a bill, passed by Congress, to bring students from the former Soviet Union countries, in an attempt to teach these future leaders about democracy. In addition to this program, there is one called YES. It brings Muslim students only. Both of these programs are currently active. In addition to FLEX, there are other scholarship programs. George Soros, a Hungarian-born, US billionaire, financier, and philanthropist, provided scholarships for high school students from Eastern European and former Soviet countries during the nineties.

Zoran was one of those students. I first met Zoran, a nonpracticing Muslim from Bosnia, in 1999. Along with his host family, I greeted him at the airport. He was seventeen and had been living with his mother, who struggled to maintain a modest home. He hadn't seen his father since he was four years old and had no siblings.

I was his area representative in name only. His hosts were the regional directors for the exchange program. According to the Federal Register Rules and Regulations, a host family can't supervise its own student. Even though Bruce and Peggy had years of experience hosting several other students, in addition to managing a twelve-state region, Zoran needed an AR. He spent his junior year in a community about sixty-five miles from Denver. His grades were excellent, and during that time, Matt, his host brother, taught him how to play tennis. He was a natural.

After the school year ended, he didn't want to return to his war-torn country. Bosnia was part of the former Yugoslavia and had been involved in civil conflict from 1992–1995. Slobodan Milosevic, Serbia's president at the time, tried to rid Bosnia of Muslims in what was referred to as "ethnic cleansing," an effort to establish a pure Serbian population that could become part of "greater Serbia."

Turning eighteen meant that Zoran would enter the military. Both his natural mother and his host family feared for his safety. In order to complete his senior year in Colorado, he would need a different kind of visa and the school would require tuition. Neither family was in a position to pay the fees. Bruce asked everyone he knew to contribute, but the undisclosed amount was still far below the tuition cost. Then he found an anonymous donor who provided the difference.

Following his high school graduation, Zoran attended a junior college and worked, while continuing to live with Peggy and Bruce. From time to time, Bruce kept me informed of Zoran's successes and failures. I knew when his host dad was proud of some choices and disappointed in others. After two years, Zoran ran out of money and was unable to continue college. He married an American woman and divorced within a year, after which Bruce and Peggy generously invited his mother and uncle to Colorado for a visit. Five years later Zoran traveled to Sarajevo for a brief stay. With the exception of the short time he was out of the country, he continued diligently playing tennis. After years of practicing and playing, he became a professional and supported himself by giving lessons.

Ten years elapsed before we met again. It was at the memorial service for Bruce, who had lost his battle with cancer. The ritualistic Catholic mass included the priest speaking about redemption while a pungent odor of incense permeated the small, modern church. After the formal service, two people spoke about Bruce. One was his son Matt and the other was Zoran, whose comments were so heartfelt there was barely a dry eye among the small group of family, neighbors, and work associates who came from around the country to pay their last respects. Zoran talked about how Bruce's voice had eased his fears during their first conversation before he left Sarajevo. He described a calm, generous man who was an excellent listener. Always, he placed others' needs before his own. Several times while Zoran was speaking, this tall, fit, stoic-looking young man became so choked up that he had to stop until he regained his composure. He paid Bruce the highest tribute when he said, "I hope that when my time comes, people will consider me, just a little bit, as fine a man as Bruce." Following the service, Zoran and I hugged, genuinely happy to see one another, but wishing it had been under different circumstances. Bruce would have been proud of Zoran that day.

Students like Zoran wouldn't have had the opportunity for such a program without scholarship aid. Mr. Soros continues to support numerous causes. His emphasis is on college students. He no longer provides high school scholarships.

The scholarship students, as well as those paying a fee, hope to improve their English. That seems to be the main goal. They also hope to experience American family life and culture. Many are motivated because they desire firsthand experience instead of what they have seen on sitcoms or in the movies.

Once or twice a year there is a "direct placement" in my region. These placements happen with American families who have a connection with a foreign family. Perhaps the Americans lived in Europe at sometime and became friendly with people who now have a teenager. The American family agrees to host their European friends' child. They still have to complete the application process. If they choose to arrange everything by themselves, the student has to pay tuition to the high school—around $8,000 for the year—because they will be coming on a different kind of visa. Generally, these placements are successful. The families know each other and have something in common.

After a family hosts a student, it is not uncommon for the same family to host a younger sibling a few years later. Some natural parents, however, don't want their second child compared to the first one. They request that the younger child be placed with a different family to create a unique experience. Sometimes they even request a different region.

In one situation, a Mexican family wanted a different American family, but the same area, for their second son. The first son, José, had spent a successful year with his family and was in a top-ranking school district. He was a skilled soccer player and was named by his team as the most valuable player of the year. When his parents came to visit the second semester, I was invited to meet them for dinner. It was a pleasant evening with delicious Mexican food, prepared by Elena, the Mexican mom. I also met the younger brothers and a sister.

Two years later José's brother, Francisco, applied for the program. Elena, who e-mailed me from time to time, asked whether I could find a home for him. I agreed to make the placement. Several months after the application process was complete, I still didn't have a placement. A family that was a good match hadn't presented itself. Finally, a family called who was interested in hosting. They had two boys who were serious soccer players. Francisco had indicated that soccer was his favorite sport. He would attend a different school than his brother, but in the same district, where the soccer team was even more competitive.

Francisco came a few weeks early to soccer camp, to improve his chances of making the team. But what if he didn't get on the team? Even worse, what if he did, but one or both of his host brothers didn't make the cut? This put some stress on the host mom, but fortunately all three boys made junior varsity. I went to one of the games. Francisco was exciting to watch. With the speed of lightning, he appeared to be all over the field at once. Like his brother José, he was named MVP by his teammates.

When soccer season was over, Francisco and his host brother continued to play for a team outside school. All in all, he had a fantastic year with his host family. Once again, Elena came for a visit, but this time without the rest of the family. It was fun to see her again. The following summer both José's and Francisco's host families were invited to the beach near Merida as guests. The three families had a delightful time. One of the host brothers remained at the beach all summer long. The youngest son will be hosted in another year by a neighbor who got to know Francisco and wants to host his brother.

In addition to placing brothers from Mexico, I also placed brothers from Germany. Over a five-year period, three brothers attended the same school. In each case, it was a direct placement, but a different host family. The German parents knew a teacher at the high school who found the first family for Maximilian. He became friendly with an American classmate whose family hosted Martin two years later. The third family hosted Moritz, having met the German parents when they were in Colorado on a visit. Each made meaningful contributions and were excellent ambassadors for their country.

Sometimes students experience dramatic changes during their American home-stay. A Jewish family hosted two Jewish students and provided positive experiences that were life-changing for Elek from Hungary, and, a few years later, Hannah from Germany. Both teens indicated in their bios that they were Jewish; neither of them, however, grew up in countries where they were comfortable identifying with Judaism. Although the host family wasn't religious, they had strong cultural connections in the Jewish community. Elek and Hannah enjoyed youth group and family events where they were exposed to their heritage. As the year progressed, and even more so when they returned to their home countries, they became comfortable with their roots.

When their host brother got married, both students returned for the wedding. Elek had completed medical school but wasn't sure what was next. Hannah worked for a while for the German organization that had sent her to the United States. She then spent a summer on a kibbutz in Israel. After that, she was a flight attendant for Lufthansa, before attending a university in Munich. Now, years later, the host family still keeps in contact with both students and has seen them several times.

Another family that remained in contact with their students was a young couple in their twenties who had hosted several students from Brazil. When they began as a host family, they didn't have children of their own. They hosted several girls and then a boy. As soon as the couple saw Ricardo's picture and bio, they knew they wanted to host him. Ricardo's long, dark hair was pulled back in a ponytail, and he indicated a deep love for music.

After his exchange student year, he stayed in Colorado and continued to live with his host family, never returning to Brazil. Ricardo had dual citizenship because he was born in the United States. Eventually his mother and younger brothers moved here to keep the family together. The host family helped them find housing and get established. Ricardo's father was already working in the United States.

Ricardo had a part-time job at a Brazilian steakhouse while he attended college. He continued to manage the restaurant after graduating and married a Brazilian woman who was living in Colorado. (Brazilians are great at networking, managing to identify all Brazilians living within a twenty-mile radius!) Several years after finishing school, Ricardo became an entrepreneur, importing fabrics and crafts from Brazil and Argentina, selling them to wholesale suppliers. Ricardo remains in contact with his host family, now the parents of two school-age boys.

In twenty years, I had only one exchange student from Egypt. Akila was a Copt, and I placed her with a Jewish family—an unlikely combination, but one that turned out well. The term *Coptic* refers to Egyptian Christians. About 10–15 percent of Egypt's population is *Coptic*, and the rest of the population is Muslim.

When Akila stepped off the plane in the summer of 1995, this dark-eyed beauty with flowing black hair looked like an Egyptian princess. She wore a midriff and tight-fitting capris that revealed her petite, perfectly proportioned figure. If the parents' thoughts were anything like mine, they were thinking that keeping the boys at bay would take some work.

In the beginning, Akila and her host family, the Goodmans, had to make some adjustments. Since the hosts were a family of five, Akila initially shared a room with one of her host sisters, which caused some problems. The host sister was used to having her own space but agreed to room with her younger sibling. Switching bedrooms so that the two host sisters were in one room and Akila in another helped to smooth out some rough spots. After a short while Akila had endeared herself to everyone.

She won the heart of her host father the evening he came home from work with some opera tickets that had been given to him by a friend. When Dan asked who wanted to go, none of his family showed any interest, except Akila. She offered to go with him. Just as they entered the Denver Center for the Arts complex on their way to the opera, a friend of Dan's spotted them. He was holding up two tickets for *Fiddler on the Roof.* It was playing in the same complex as the opera. He explained that he couldn't use his tickets, which were third row center, and wondered if they would like them. It didn't take Dan and Akila long to say, "Yes!"—preferring the play to the opera. They loved the play, the music, and the evening they spent together.

At the end of the year, several members of Akila's family came to Colorado to meet the host family and make the return trip to Egypt with Akila. Her mother, grandmother, and two siblings came and stayed with the Goodmans for three weeks. The two families bonded so well that over the years they traveled back and forth between Cairo and Denver many times. When the Goodmans son became a Bar Mitzvah, the families met in Israel. And when their daughter became a Bat Mitzvah, the Egyptian family came to Colorado for the celebration. Naomi, the host mom, has been to Egypt three times, one being the occasion of Akila's wedding, when all the Goodmans attended.

Shortly after 9/11, air travel wasn't comfortable for many Americans, let alone a Jewish family traveling to the Middle East. With some hesitation, Dan took his family to Cairo. Akila's dad impressed upon Dan how important their attendance at his daughter's wedding was to him. Once again, he gratefully thanked Dan for taking such good care of his daughter for a year. At the wedding, they played "Sunrise, Sunset" from *Fiddler on the Roof,* which was Akila's favorite music. More than a few tears were shed. Both families joyously sang and danced to the familiar tunes. The last I heard, the parents, Akila, her husband, and two children had moved to Dubai, and Naomi, the host mom, was going to visit them.

In 1992, on the other side of Asia, when the government in China eased their laws and began releasing baby girls for adoption, Americans began adopting Chinese babies. According to the US State Department, only a few hundred were adopted in the United States the first year, but that number increased to the thousands. By 2005, 14,500 Chinese babies were adopted, with United States citizens having adopted more than 70%. When those babies reached school age, the parents were eager for their adopted daughters to learn something about their cultural heritage.

The Smiths had an eleven-year-old Chinese daughter whom they adopted as a baby when they decided to host Lei, who came from a rural area in Yu Nan province. When Lei arrived at the airport, her appearance reminded me of Raggedy Ann; she had shaggy, black hair and lips that turned up slightly at the corners. She wore blue denim overalls that came just above her knees and was clutching a medium-sized teddy bear. Assuming that the bear was for her host sister would have been inaccurate. This was Lei's bear, and it was her security blanket. She wasn't about to let it go.

A few days later, another sixteen-year-old Chinese girl arrived at the airport. Fan wore high-heeled, pointy-toed shoes, large, dangling earrings, and a chic outfit. Her small build belied her confidence. She didn't wait for her host family at the assigned meeting place but went to claim her belongings. I found her at the baggage carousel. Fan was perky and poised, even though she had been traveling for hours.

The two girls may both have been from China, but they were from different regions and had little in common. They reminded me of one of my favorite childhood books, *The City Mouse-Country Mouse,* based on an Aesop folktale. In spite of their differences, Fan and Lei become close friends during the year they were here. They lived at opposite ends of the Denver area, but their host families arranged for the two girls to spend time together, which they delighted in doing. A little touch of home from time to time is comforting for exchange students.

Fan shared with her host mother that it is common in China to be an only child. Americans hear about the one-child rule but fail to take it one step further. If both parents are only children, there are no aunts, uncles, or cousins. They have no extended family except possibly doting grandparents. Fan didn't live at home because the school in her little village didn't provide her with an education that promised any future. Instead she attended school in the city and saw her parents on weekends. She didn't have close friends at school because of competition for a spot at a university. According to Fan, teens don't develop a trusting relationship with their peers. They are afraid to share their hopes and dreams and will never tell another student their grades.

In 2008, six months after hearing this story, I attended an all-day symposium on China, given by Dr. Jonathan Adelman, a full professor in the graduate school of International Relations at Denver University. He had just returned from his eighteenth trip to China. According to Professor Adelman, the one-child rule is still enforced unless both parents are only children; then two babies are permitted. He told us that almost 50 percent of university students are females, a recent change. A year later, I visited China and heard about the one-child policy, but I learned that more children are permitted in rural areas and to minority groups.

Shortly before my China trip, I had lunch with Yu, a Chinese graduate student who was attending Denver University on a partial scholarship, provided by private funds. She said the brightest Chinese students are in the United States going to college. Yu, an only child, expressed her desire to stay in the United States, but she will return to China to take care of her parents when they get older. She honors her obligation to her parents.

In China, even with girls having more opportunities to enter good universities and secure jobs following graduation, the competition is great. They often don't want to return to their home country because they believe that there are more opportunities for success in the United

States. The Chinese sending partner representative assures that this won't happen by collecting their passports and visas when they step off the plane in California. These are returned when they leave ten months later.

In another instance, Hurgen, a Mongolian boy, applied through another partner, who did not collect the passports. Hurgen was a mature student and was given the responsibility for his own passport's safe keeping. During the year he got along quite well with his host family, made a number of friends, and earned excellent grades. Two weeks before the end of the program, he washed his jeans with his passport in the back pocket. All the writing was erased, rendering the passport blank. It took some time to get a new one, delaying his return. I never knew for sure whether this was an honest mistake or he knew this would happen. Without a passport, he couldn't return to Mongolia. Eventually, Hurgen left Denver on a flight to San Francisco, where he was to board his flight for Ulaanbaatar, the capital city. He managed to meet another passenger with whom he became acquainted on the flight to San Francisco and remained in California for an extended period of time. Usually students return to their home country when school is out in early June. Sigfried, a German girl, extended her stay because the host couple was expecting a baby in mid-June, and she wanted to wait until the baby was born so that she could help.

I always ask the exchange students to do a volunteer project while they are in the United States. It is usually a family project. Students occasionally get involved through their host family's church. Other students assist the teacher in their language class or offer to tutor after school. One

Spanish girl enjoyed reading to children in the hospital. She told me that she was going to go to a hospital when she returned to Spain and insist that they let her volunteer. Volunteerism isn't as common in other countries as it is in America. Students observe that Americans are generous, not only by hosting, but by giving of their time.

As much as volunteerism is encouraged, work requiring a social security number is not permitted. Students can earn extra money by babysitting, pet sitting, tutoring, shoveling snow, or doing yard work, as long as they don't work more than ten hours a week. For the most part, they are too busy with schoolwork and extracurricular activities, but sometimes they want to earn some extra spending money, and that is permissible.

Max, a German student, and his host dad went to a small town in Mexico. In connection with their church, they built an entire house for a poor family through Habitat for Humanity. The house was completed in less than two weeks. Kai had the most interesting volunteer job. She offered to train a seeing-eye dog. Kai didn't have any experience with dogs and didn't even have a pet in her home in Japan. It was a tremendous undertaking. Brandy, a yellow Labrador retriever, had to go everywhere she went because he could never be left alone. After several months, the host mom began taking the dog to work with her so that Kai, who had responsibly taken the dog to school every day, could participate in some other activities and have a well-rounded experience. It turned out that the dog was difficult to train and not a good candidate to be a seeing-eye dog. After several more months, Brandy was rejected from the program. Kai, on the other hand, proved to be an exceptional exchange student and was chosen by her peers to represent them by giving a speech at graduation, even though she herself wasn't graduating.

Once in a while, I would meet a student at the airport whose personality spoke of success. Lena was such a student. Although Lena came from Germany, her parents were born in Iran. When she deplaned, as exhausted as the other students, her bouncy gait exuded confidence and enthusiasm. She arrived with more than the usual one or two large suitcases and a backpack. She also had her violin and her snowboard. True to my first impression, her year was successful in all regards. She played the violin for the school orchestra, achieved good grades, made many friends, enjoyed her host mother, and got the most from her experience. She was the quintessential applicant. Lena was an example of a student who was self-reliant and required less intervention to succeed.

Exchange students come from all over the world and are placed in homes throughout the United States. Successful exchange students, like successful host families, are adaptable and communicative. I have shown numerous examples of international students who have established such close ties that they are now treated like family members. They continue to visit their host families and invite their families to visit them.

Chapter 4

Schools—The Branches

Host families provide the roots or foundation, the students the variety, and the school the opportunity for a student to learn, branch out, and grow. When you purchase a young tree in a container, it looks like not much more than a stick, but as it establishes itself in the ground the roots begin to spread. The spread of a tree's roots is equal to the spread of its branches.

When exchange students feel a part of their host families, become more comfortable with their English and are getting over their culture shock, they are ready to expand their experiences. Attending school is an essential part of the academic semester or year program. The first weeks of school are always an adjustment because schools in the countries from which we accept students are quite different than American schools. It is important to understand the differences so that a host family or school counselor can help their exchange student to adjust. In many cases, students begin school and graduate with the same classmates. In other countries, students stay in the same classroom all day, and the teachers move. Imagine a student who is used to this system, trying to navigate in a school of over three thousand! First period his class may be on the first floor and second period on the third.

Then, too, a high school student in the United States might take biology as a sophomore, chemistry as a junior, and physics as a senior. Brazilians take all three sciences every year throughout high school. It is customary to take twelve academic courses, but every subject isn't taught every day. Another difference is the total number of years required to graduate. The Latin American countries frequently require eleven years. In Germany, the academic track students who attend the gymnasium must complete thirteen years. That has recently changed to twelve in some states. German students who aren't planning to attend college graduate high school after ten years. Italians and Norwegians require thirteen years. Some of the exchange students receive credit for their time in the United States. Spain, Mexico, Italy, and Brazil, for example, don't require their students to repeat the year if they take a specified curriculum. The notarized transcript is sent in a sealed envelope to the consulate from the student's country. It is stamped with an *apostille*, a raised seal, which certifies the authenticity of the signature on the transcript and is required for international acceptance. This is a necessary procedure before the student can reenter school in her home country. Other students participate simply for the experience, knowing that they will have to repeat the year when they return. In some cases, if they can pass a test when they go back, they can continue to the next level.

Schools also start at different times of the year throughout the world. In Japan the school year begins in March. In Brazil it begins in February, and summer vacation is in December and January because the seasons there are the opposite of ours.

Exchange students are encouraged to get involved in extracurricular activities, since this is a good way for them to make American friends. They may see someone in their first-hour class with whom they would like to make friends, and then not see them the rest of the day. If they are in an activity, it is more likely that they will get to know someone with the same interest.

The United States is unique in offering extracurricular activities as part of the school experience. In other countries, schools are for classes only. There is no social life or opportunity for sports. Any extra activity is done privately after school, not as a part of the school day, so many exchange students take advantage of the opportunity to play sports and join clubs.

Anyone who joins a club and pays for a sport in his home country is guaranteed that he can participate. It was upsetting to Ricardo, from Brazil, when he got onto the school baseball team, only to be cut a week later. The team was extremely competitive, with many outstanding players. Ricardo had never played baseball before and wasn't as good as the American kids. He didn't understand that just wanting to play wasn't good enough. After getting over the disappointment, he tried out for track, where he was assured that he could continue to participate.

Lisa had a similar experience with volleyball. She had played the game for years in Germany, but never seriously. After making the team, she was cut after a few weeks. She commented about how competitive Americans are when it comes to sports.

Other students are outstanding athletes, and school coaches are delighted to have them as participants. Guilia, a Brazilian, was the best girl's tennis player her school had ever had. There were dozens of soccer players who excelled, including one or two who took their teams to state. The girls enjoy getting on the volleyball and swim teams; the boys like cross-country, soccer, and lacrosse.

Participating in sports is easier than getting speaking parts in the class plays because of limited English. Many get dancing roles or sing in the chorus. Others work on the sets, makeup, costumes, lighting, and staging. One girl played Nana, the dog, in *Peter Pan*. Several played in the orchestra. Kim, from South Korea, who played for her school performances, came back to the United States on a full college scholarship to study piano.

Linda, a tall, slender, beautiful girl from Norway was such a talented flutist that her orchestra teacher suggested she try out for All-State Band. When I congratulated Linda for being nominated, she told me that she didn't think she would make it to the finals. In fact, she was accepted and performed at a college with other students from throughout the state. Without much effort, she earned first chair, to the dismay of some other students who were much more serious about their music. Every few months, I called the school counselor to see how the exchange students were doing. According to her counselor, Linda was an outstanding ambassador for her country. At the completion of the year, Linda received several musical honors. Even though she was obviously a talented musician, Linda thought that music would be her avocation. Art was her passion.

One activity unique to the United States is prom. None of the exchange students know anything about this event until they get here. Almost all of them want to participate. If they don't get a date, they go as a group or at least go to after-prom. When spring break ends, the boys are already considering whom they will ask. The actual date differs in each school, but the prom is held on a weekend night in April or May. It is an expensive evening. By the time a boy rents a tux, makes sure he has the right shoes, shirt, and tie, shares the rental of a limo, buys a corsage, pays for dinner and photos, he's spent several hundred dollars. The girls have to buy a gown and shoes, get their hair and nails done, and buy a boutonniere, but the boys incur the greatest expense. Following the event, when I ask them if they had a good time, the usual response is a shrug and the comment that the anticipation and planning were better than the prom itself. The more popular part of the evening is after-prom, and it is free. Schools vary the activities provided at after-prom, but generally there is free food, games, music, and photos. Parents plan and chaperone the event. Junior and senior students may attend even if they don't attend prom.

My favorite school in which to place exchange students was one that assigns an American friend to each international girl or boy. The exchange student has someone to shadow. They are escorted to their classrooms and don't have to worry about eating lunch alone. It is such a great idea that I always hope other schools will implement the same plan.

Some teachers extend themselves to ensure that exchange students have a successful experience. For years, the teacher who created the American friend idea also dedicated an entire week to foreign students from around the state. She arranged housing with host families. The event was called World Awareness Week. Students of the same nationality taught classes about their country to the American teens. Guest speakers were invited to give presentations. The week culminated with a dinner that was prepared by the exchange students and skits that represented each ethnicity.

Extra activities are important, but grades are even more important. Students are expected to maintain a C average. If they get an F they are required to get tutoring, at their own expense, in the subject they are failing. Sometimes another student is available to tutor for a nominal fee. Keeping schools happy with our students assures slots for the future. Most of the exchange students get excellent grades. Tranh, from Vietnam, scored the highest in math of any student who had ever attended his high school of close to four thousand. Regardless of nationality, the students feel that American schools are easier than schools in other countries. Frequently they would tell me that the material they were currently studying had been covered in their home school a grade or so earlier.

If a student continues to get poor grades or is expelled from school for any reason, his program is terminated, and he is immediately repatriated (the term used when a student is sent home at his own expense). In my more than twenty years in the field, I saw less than a handful expelled. An exception was Bruno, a well-mannered Brazilian boy, with a pleasant, easy manner and good grades. He was well liked by his host family, teachers, AR, and the other students. Bruno was attending a large suburban high school. Late in the fall semester, his chemistry class was studying combustion, and they were required to bring matches to class one day.

Later that evening, Bruno had basketball practice in the school gym. His host father had a meeting, so he brought Bruno back to school a little before practice was to start. An immature, bored, sixteen-year-old with time on his hands spells trouble. Strolling the halls, hands in his pockets, waiting for practice to begin, he rediscovered the matches. He began striking them, blowing them out, and throwing them into a trash can in the hall. Bruno repeated this until all the remaining matches were lit. After a while, smoke starting spewing out of the can. Transfixed, Bruno nervously watched the events unfold. Apparently, the smoke set off the fire alarm, and the building was speedily evacuated. Within minutes, sirens blared as they approached the school. Fire trucks arrived, and firemen hoisting hoses entered the school, quickly dampening the smoke. Soon after, the fireman left, and once again the building was occupied. Bruno never went to practice that night. Pacing nervously, he waited until his host father picked him up. Driving home, he quietly sat in the passenger seat, saying nothing about the evening's events. The next morning he began telling his host mom an abbreviated version of the previous evening's occurrences when the phone rang. It was a school official informing the host mother that Bruno was in big trouble. The entire incident had been captured on the school surveillance camera. There was no resolution. Since the school had a zero-tolerance policy, Bruno was expelled. Expulsion meant repatriation.

A few days later, I drove Bruno to the airport for his morning flight to São Paulo because his host parents were working. Bruno and I were both sad and disappointed, knowing he was not a bad kid, but that poor judgment had caused a bleak outcome. He learned a painful lesson. When I asked him how this would have been handled in Brazil, he was convinced that he would have been reprimanded, not expelled. He had difficulty with the harsh decision. The following year, his parents invited his host family to Brazil. Bruno and his parents showed them a wonderful time. Not one word was ever mentioned about the fateful incident.

Occasionally, there is an episode in school where the student is involved but is not responsible. On a cold February morning, I got a call from Jane, a host mother who was with her exchange student at the emergency room. In a morning PE class, Sven, from Sweden, was participating in a basketball game. Sven caught the ball, which angered Calvin, an American student. Both boys were down on the floor, tussling for the ball. When it became apparent that Sven, now in a fetal position clutching the ball, had possession, Calvin proceeded to land several punches to Sven's head and rib cage. The coach and four classmates witnessed the assault. It all happened in a flash. When the teacher broke it up, Calvin walked away uttering a biased ethnic slur. Sven's host mother was notified, and she came to the school and took Sven to a nearby hospital where a CT scan revealed that he had a concussion. There were no broken bones. Rest and a few days off school were the doctor's orders. Sven didn't even know Calvin. He had done nothing to provoke him, which was substantiated by all four witnesses in the police report.

The host parents were distressed. They felt embarrassed to have to call Sven's parents in Sweden and tell them of this unfortunate incident. A host family feels responsible for the safety of their student. Jane and Robert had done everything imaginable to provide a safe and positive experience for Sven. As a result of this incident, however, a stronger bond was created between Sven and his host parents.

Calvin received a temporary suspension from school. After a hearing, with his parents present, he was allowed to return to school with mandatory counseling. Because this was his first offense and it was a misdemeanor, not a felony, he wasn't expelled. This was the school policy. I asked what would have made it a felony and was told it would have been a felony had there been a weapon involved or had Sven sustained more serious injuries. The host family was assured that the two boys wouldn't have any classes together the remainder of the year. Sven didn't allow this incident to mar his otherwise positive experience. He hoped for an apology but never got one. Fortunately, the school year ended without further incident. The last week of school, Sven was issued a subpoena to appear in court. One hour before the scheduled court appearance, Jane received a call that Calvin had pleaded guilty. It was unnecessary for Sven to go to court. I was not privy to Calvin's sentence, if any.

In a shocking incident at Columbine High School, my concern was for Isabella, a Spanish student who was attending the school. Americans old enough to remember have vivid memories of where they were and how they felt when they learned that President Kennedy had been assassinated, and on 9/11, when the twin towers fell. I can add to that list the Columbine School shootings. On April 20, 1999, two teenagers, Eric Harris and Dylan Klebold, marched into the school, killing twelve students, one teacher, and themselves in the worst American high school attack to that date.

The day started out warm and sunny. By the time I drove home from work that afternoon, it had started to rain. Turning onto my street, I realized that my neighborhood had experienced a spring snowstorm. The heavy, wet snow blanketed the spring green lawns. My focus was on getting home safely. Dinner and a quiet evening followed. Typically I turn on the TV to watch the 10:00 p.m. news, but for some reason I went straight to bed, not knowing that the Littleton community and all of Colorado was devastated and in shock.

At breakfast, while reading the morning paper, details and pictures revealed the carnage of this hideous tragedy. Stunned, I read page after page, trying to absorb the contents. Tears trickled down my cheeks and then I began to experience panic. Isabella's name was not listed as a victim, so I knew she was alive, but I didn't know any details.

Isabella had two host sisters who also attended Columbine. Later I learned that one of her sisters was the last one to leave the cafeteria alive. Neither Isabella nor her host sisters had been physically harmed, but they were suffering emotional anguish. The school was closed and would remain closed for the remainder of the school year. Students finished the year at a neighboring school.

It seemed likely that Isabella would return to Spain at her earliest opportunity; that was not the case, however. Having become part of her host family, community, and school, all of whom were in mourning and grappling with the events, she chose to stay. Isabella needed time to deal with the devastation and horror. She wanted to offer support to her host sisters and have them support her. Isabella's mother wanted her daughter to come home to Spain. Telephone calls went back and forth between Isabella and her mother. The host family was so distraught that the AR, although supportive, didn't want to impose by calling too frequently. A few weeks later, I learned that Isabella's mother had come from Spain and was also living in the house. With all the emotion and sadness this family was dealing with, they were able to welcome another person into their home. Isabella and her mother returned to Spain, but not for several weeks.

Hundreds, if not thousands, of exchange students attend high school every day and finish their year without incident, making lasting contributions. Earning good grades, making American friends, and participating in extracurricular activities are the goals. The students consider it the best year of their lives. Only the few bizarre and unusual situations are reported and remembered. It is important to realize that these are the exceptions.

Chapter 5

The Area Representative—Placement and Support

Selecting the right tree for the right spot is exceedingly important. One must consider the size of the tree at maturity. Space, views, proximity to the house, property lines, location of underground utilities as well as overhead wires are a few of the factors that must be weighed to determine the best placement. If a tree is uprooted once established, the sensitive root hairs are damaged, and once again the tree is in shock. Likewise, if a student requires a new placement, she experiences rejection and is plummeted into a new situation, and she must adjust all over again. The goal is to place the student once.

The area representative constitutes the fourth part of the exchange, along with the host family, student, school, and organization. Liking teenagers, good community contacts, and counseling skills are important qualifications for an AR. An experienced AR spends time getting to know host families and what they are looking for in the way of an exchange student. As I previously mentioned, it is the AR who determines, after an in-home interview and reference check, whether a family is suitable for hosting and whether to make a placement.

There are many reasons families have for wanting a student. It is up to the AR to make sure it is a healthy reason rather than a dysfunctional one. The first responsibility of the AR is to identify families interested in hosting. This is accomplished through networking, former host families, and leads that come through churches, schools, or the Internet. Once interest is indicated, the AR makes contact by phone before scheduling a home visit. At the time of the interview, all host family members eighteen years of age or older do their own criminal background check so that the AR won't be privy to the family's private information, such as social security numbers. The AR provides them with an Internet site. Any criminal charge is reported back to the exchange program national office. The initial visit takes about two hours. Afterward the AR checks references, completes paperwork, and makes sure that the selected student hasn't been placed elsewhere. A signed school permission form giving the student permission to attend is obtained by the AR.

Additionally, the AR provides supervision and counseling when needed. At times intervention is not only necessary, but saves placements that are floundering. Two examples come to mind. Sitting around a dining room table, I once facilitated a discussion with a host family consisting of a mother, father, teenage daughter, younger son, and their Argentine exchange student, Marco. Expressing the crux of the problem was the daughter, who was bearing the brunt of responsibility. Sheila's parents had burdened her with driving Marco everywhere he needed to go and including him in all her after-school activities. One by one, each person shared his or her frustrations. As soon as I reiterated that no one person was responsible for the exchange student, the atmosphere in the room lightened. Marco was happy that he would have some time to himself and an opportunity to make some of his own friends. The parents realized that they had had unrealistic expectations of their daughter and apologized. Sheila visibly showed relief that she could do some things without Marco and not feel guilty. The remainder of the year went on without a hitch.

The second example where intervention salvaged a placement involved an unhappy mother who was angered by continuous teasing and sarcasm dished out by Angelo, the Italian boy they were hosting. It seemed only to be directed toward Marcie, the mom. She found him rude and insensitive to her feelings. The host dad worked long hours, and when he came home, his wife unloaded complaints about Angelo. After a while he became resentful. Tired and unhappy to come home to a barrage of complaints, he chose to ignore them and withdraw from any interaction with Angelo. The host brother was the same age as Angelo and got along well with his new sibling. They enjoyed each other like brothers, sometimes disagreeing, but mostly comfortable with one another. This relationship steadied the placement for a while.

When I first learned of the problem, I suggested that Marcie confront Angelo and tell him what she didn't like and tell him to stop. She insisted that she had done so, without success. Involving the natural mother had little effect. She was a single mom who may have had a similar dynamic with her only son. When Angelo acted rudely, Marcie retaliated with verbal outbursts. The situation was getting ugly, so I offered to meet with them. Some long phone conversations with each individual solved the problem. I strongly urged the host father to talk firmly to Angelo, and I did the same. When the host dad sat Angelo down and spelled out what had to happen, Angelo insisted that he hadn't realized the effect he was having on his host mom. He told me the same thing. He was happy in the placement and didn't want to jeopardize it. Genuinely sorry for his inappropriate teasing, he dramatically changed his behavior and attitude. Marcie couldn't believe the difference. When I called, weeks and months later, to check on things, she would say that he was a different person, acting like a normal kid. They were engaging in meaningful conversations, going skiing or snowboarding, and acting like a family.

Anytime a student or family experiences an adjustment issue or a problem that necessitates moving a student to a new family, it is the AR who is responsible. For this reason, some organizations require representatives to have bimonthly contact with the family and student, even though the Department of State requires only monthly communication. Presently, the AR cannot live more than 120 miles away, although this may be changing. For more serious issues, the local representative has the support of the regional director and the national office.

Determining whether the problem is cultural, a personality clash, sibling resentment, or lack of communication is the first step. If the student moves to a new family, the interview and application process have to be repeated prior to the student relocation.

Every year 10–12 percent of the students in our region move to a new family for one reason or another, sometimes the result of a work transfer or illness. It isn't always a student or family problem. Our region had fewer moves than the national average. I credit this to a caring, experienced team of ARs who matched appropriate students and provided support. Good supervision prevents small problems from becoming big ones. Recognizing when intervention is necessary may salvage a troubled placement. Phoning the student and meeting for orientations is required, though our region planned activities and met with the students throughout the year, as the sample schedule in Chapter 3 demonstrated. Detailed information can be found in Chapter 8.

Chapter 6

Fall Travel Perks for ARs—Autumn Leaves

One of the beauties of fall is the splendor of deciduous trees, with their dazzling display of colorful leaves. Autumn offers a perk for ARs: the opportunity to travel as a guest of the exchange program. In October or November, the staff, managers, and ARs who qualify are invited to attend the yearly conference. Most representatives have regular jobs and place students as an avocation. ARs receive a stipend, but every placement also yields points toward travel. A certain number of points earn an invitation to the annual conference.

These meetings are stimulating, motivational, and fun. Seeing people once a year from all over the United States is like a big reunion. Locations alternate between an American city and a European or Latin American locale. When the conference is in the United States, it lasts four days. Meetings out of the country last for five days. The conferences enable representatives to meet the foreign sending partners and hear speakers talk about cultural differences. ARs become acquainted with the problems the partners face when working with the natural parents. These inspirational speakers and informative meetings offer firsthand opportunities to increase cultural awareness.

For instance, at the conference in Barcelona, we heard an influential speaker who had a strong impact and increased our understanding. Luby Ismail, president and founder of Connecting Cultures Inc., is a middle-aged Muslim woman with dark hair and a slight build who remained seated during most of her presentation. She is an engaging speaker who talked about growing up in Florida, attempting to dispel myths American women have about Islamic women. About thirty minutes into her presentation, when she had captivated her mostly female audience and had them in the palm of her hand, she asked everyone to close their eyes and keep them closed until they were told to open them. In a few minutes they saw that she had donned a *hijab*, a loose scarf worn over the head and under the chin by some Muslim women. It resulted in a shock effect, silencing the room. This was precisely the reaction she expected. She then asked the audience how they felt when they saw her wearing the *hijab*. Hands flew up, and women gave responses like submissiveness, sadness, lack of equality, and discomfort. The speaker nodded at the responses but made no comment and continued for the next thirty minutes with her presentation. By the end of the hour, her admirers had once again become comfortable and engaged in listening to what she had to say, instead of focusing on her head scarf and what it represented. Following each keynote speaker there is a break that allows time for members of the audience to discuss how they feel and what they have learned. Unanimously, the group agreed that a barrier was removed, allowing for greater understanding between Muslims and non-Muslims.

At a conference in Washington, DC, the keynote speaker spoke about task versus relationship. According to Gary R. Weaver from American University, "When cultures collide, it's not a matter of different behavior but rather a clash of different values, beliefs, way of thinking, and worldviews. Americans are a to-do society rather than a to-be." Americans are task oriented. Getting the job done is more important than the relationship with the person with whom you are working. In Latin American, the relationship is more important than getting something accomplished.

Breaks at the annual conference provide time for touring and socializing. The culmination of the meeting is an awards ceremony, followed by a farewell dinner. Phil and I always extended our stay, traveling independently or with other ARs, visiting nearby areas. Many of the venues are selected because we place their students. Becoming more familiar with the cultures helps with student interaction.

Following a conference in Hawaii, Phil and I decided to visit Kyoto, Japan. It was the year that Kai was in Denver. She is the Japanese girl who volunteered to train Brandy, the seeing-eye dog. Kai arranged for us to have a meeting with her parents. They came from Osaka to Kyoto by train and then walked a long distance to the small, business-class hotel where we were staying. When we met Kai's mother and father in the lobby, we were surprised to see her grandmother and brother too. They welcomed us warmly and presented us with gifts before taking us out to dinner. Our hotel wasn't far from the geisha district called *Gion*, the place of origin of Kabuki, a form of Japanese drama begun in the late 1500s. We crossed the bridge over the Kamogawa River, walking through a neighborhood of teahouses, department stores, and specialty shops.

Several blocks farther on we arrived at a *ryocan*, a traditional Japanese inn that serves exotic food and offers elegant lodging. We were ushered into a small, private dining room, separated from other rooms by Japanese shoji screens. There was one windowed wall facing a narrow, enclosed walkway. The low, rectangular table, flanked by a bench on each side, seated the six of us. For the next few hours, we dined on a typical *kaiseki* meal that had half a dozen courses. The presentation seemed as important as the ingredients. Each course was beautifully served in different bowls with elaborate garnishes. Some serving dishes were ceramic pottery, others porcelain or lacquer, each meant to complement the food.

The ambiance was intended to be relaxing, but everything was unfamiliar and communication was strained, so I felt a little anxious. The Japanese father had a language translator, but it made little difference. When I asked him what we were eating, he quickly typed some letters into the computer, looked up, smiled, and gave me the translation. Even with the English words, I sometimes didn't recognize the ingredients. For example, one dish was made with lotus root and several with raw fish that had strange-sounding names. When the tofu, which had a stringy, more liquid consistency than I was used to, kept slipping between my chopsticks, the grandmother spoke some Japanese to the waiter, and in an instant we were presented with spoons and forks. Amused, and slightly embarrassed, I was determined to master chopsticks. Phil appreciated the practicality and gratefully switched to the more familiar utensils.

The dinner was magical, as was the entire evening spent with Kai's family. Catching a fleeting glimpse of a geisha through the window while we were dining was a highlight. I had just finished reading *Memoirs of a Geisha* and was fascinated by these beautiful women with powdered, white faces. They wear silk kimonos, are talented in conversation and dance, and have the ability to play several musical instruments. After dinner, we walked through lighted gardens, passing shrines and temples, before returning to the hotel.

For days and weeks after visiting Kyoto, I digested and reflected on this exotic experience, recognizing my deepening love for cultural diversity. Prior to this trip I hadn't appreciated the homogeneity of Japan. Everywhere I looked, Toyotas filled the busy streets. People were dressed the same. All the school children wore uniforms consisting of navy blue blazers and white shirts, girls with skirts and boys with pants. Businessmen also wore navy blue blazers. Everyone had straight, black hair, even elderly people. Apparently, many women dye their hair. My white hair, height, and dress singled me out as an American.

Some school children approached us at one of the shrines and asked if they could practice their English. In a rote, mechanical way, reading from a notebook, they began asking questions. Of course, I was delighted to engage them and smiled when they haltingly asked Phil, "Are you a grandpa?" Additionally, I was struck by the politeness and helpfulness of the Japanese. Frequently we would be standing on a street corner, studying our map, looking lost or confused, and someone would stop to help us.

One morning, we had taken a train ride to the ancient city of Nara, about an hour from Kyoto. Finding our way there was easy. After spending several hours enjoying the shrine and the tame deer, who came right up to us and posed until their picture was taken, we decided it was time to return to Kyoto. We had gotten turned around, however, and couldn't figure out the way back to the train. After walking around in circles for what seemed like a long time, I spotted some tour buses. I approached a man, probably the driver, waiting alongside a bus for his group. He spoke no English, although with the use of our map and a lot of gesturing, he seemed to understand where we needed to go in order to catch our return train. It appeared that we had veered quite a distance in the wrong direction. Fifteen minutes later, this kind man had walked us all the way to our stop. We offered to pay him, but he refused. I hope we hadn't offended him. When we got back to Colorado, I sent a gift to the Japanese family, and we took Kai and her friend to an authentic Japanese restaurant that we all enjoyed.

One exotic conference destination was Barcelona, a cosmopolitan Spanish city on the Mediterranean Sea. One would think it an ideal location to practice her Spanish; even though Spanish is spoken, Catalonian is the official language. Our group quickly learned that in Spain, dinner isn't served until 10:00 p.m. Restaurants don't even open until 9:00 p.m. or later. Sampling *tapas*, paella, and sangria while watching flamenco introduced us to the region of bullfights and toreadors. Street performers are a common sight on the famous pedestrian street called The Ramblas. Human statues remain mute and perfectly still until someone tosses a coin into a small container. At that time they come alive and perform for a minute or two; then they became human statues again. Crowds stroll the outdoor street malls watching the entertainers until midnight, usually later.

My favorite conference was held at a beach resort near Salvador, Brazil, in the northeastern state of Bahia, where it is warm, often hot, all year. Four million people live in this exotic city, the third largest in Brazil. A colonial city built on two levels, Salvador was the first capital of Brazil and has a strong African influence. It is estimated that 4.5 million African slaves were brought to Salvador. That represents three times the number of slaves who came to North America.

One evening our group traveled to this lively city by bus. We had dinner and watched a typical Brazilian show. Dancing, singing, laughter, and blaring instruments are all part of a typical evening. After the meeting, some of the ARs spent several additional days immersing themselves in the culture. The smells of pungent spices and local foods permeate the air as the crowds inch past open-air restaurants and markets. Spicy, West African seafood dishes prepared with palm oil are popular with the natives. Hordes of scantily clad, cinnamon-colored natives of all ages jam the streets late at night and into the early morning.

At one point, the ARs stopped to watch some *capoeira* performers who had attracted a sizable crowd. *Capoeira* is a combination of dance and martial art requiring strength and dexterity. It originated with the slaves in Salvador and helped to boost their morale. One can't help but feel the rhythm of the music and try to emulate the dancers with swaying hips and moving feet. Seated at a restaurant frequented by the natives, and open to the street, we were able to sample the local cuisine, watch the crowds, listen to the music, and experience the sensuality of Salvador.

Here, as well as in other large cities in Brazil, people live in small apartments without patios and gardens. Inviting guests to one's home isn't practical. Brazilians are sociable; meeting friends and family outdoors is part of the culture. The climate is mild enough all year to meet nightly. Although they are used to warm weather, Brazilians love to come to Colorado. In most cases, they have never seen snow—at least not in Brazil—and they want the experience. Having an opportunity to ski or snowboard thrills them, though they complain about the cold weather.

When a Brazilian student comes from Salvador, Rio de Janeiro, or São Paulo and is placed in a suburb or a town of several hundred or even a few thousand, she frequently experiences a difficult adjustment. Culture shock is inevitable. My trip to Brazil helped me to understand how a lifestyle where one spends much of the year outdoors and meets with friends almost nightly works in Brazil, but not in the United States.

Marcelo, from Brazil, commented, "I thought that the US was the land of freedom, but you have way more rules than we do." He was referring to the curfew for teenagers. He didn't understand why he had to be home by 10:00 p.m. on a school night and by midnight on the weekend. His host parents were enforcing safety and obeying the law. In Brazil, his natural parents understood that he might not be home until 1:00 a.m. or later because neither would they.

In 2008, Costa Rica, an environmentally conscious country, was the venue for the conference. One day, instead of sitting in traditional meetings, fifty staff members and area representatives, aided by local *Ticos*—what the people from Costa Rica call themselves—planted two hundred saplings in an effort to reforest an area void of vegetation. My team worked together successfully for years. In addition to the satisfaction and gratification they received from working with host families and exchange students, the ARs appreciated the opportunity to attend the fall conferences.

Chapter 7

Exchange Program Organization—The Arborist

An arborist is a tree specialist, responsible for the health and maintenance of trees. Arborists evaluate and determine whether the tree requires pruning, fertilizing, replanting, or replacing. Exchange organizations sustain and preserve the health of the program. National offices are staffed with workers who provide the necessary functions to ensure that everything runs smoothly. In addition, the national office maintains the well-being of the field staff. They hire and train personnel.

The Department of State determines the requirements, and CSIET sets the standards for exchange programs. The organization meets the standards necessary for accreditation and ensures annual listing. Federal Register guidelines must be met. As an example, since 2006 the Department of State requires that all sponsors perform a criminal background check on all employees and representatives, as well as host families.

All student applications are sent to the national office. A staff member reads the applications, making sure they are complete. She translates the grades, determines that immunizations are current and photos included and then uploads the information onto the database.

Organizations in the United States work with sending partners throughout the world. Students come on a J-1 visa designation, which is issued for a maximum of one year and can't be renewed. This visa allows students to attend public school tuition-free. The sponsor provides the necessary documents to apply for the J-l visa. An essential requirement for receiving a J-1 visa is obtaining a DS-2019 form. The accredited sponsoring organization sends the DS-2019 to the sending partner. When the applicant has the necessary paperwork, they go for an interview. Following the interview at the American Embassy in the student's country, the J-1 visa is issued. Sometimes applicants are rejected.

Students, host families, and area representatives complete evaluations three times a year. They are reviewed at the regional level and then sent to the national office. The exchange organization sends them to the partners in each country. Subsequently, they are forwarded to the natural parents. Any serious student issues are handled by the national office.

As well as the academic semester and year-long programs, there are summer, short-term, and outbound opportunities. All programs originate and are organized at the national level. The executives in the exchange organizations have wisdom and experience, enabling them to make good decisions that promote the success of the programs. They decide when to cut, reduce, or add staff and applicants. Another responsibility is identifying new sending partners and new countries to assure continued growth.

Chapter 8

The Calendar—Tree Rings

We learned as children that a tree's age is easily determined by counting its growth rings. Annually, the tree adds new layers of wood, which thicken during the growing season and thin during the winter. These annual growth rings are easily countable in cross sections of the tree's trunk. This is the case in parts of the world with distinct seasons. When I visited a cloud forest in Costa Rica, I viewed the cross section of the trunk of an old tree that had been toppled by a storm, and I didn't see any rings. The local guide explained that trees there don't have rings because they don't experience seasons.

The exchange student's year begins in August, about one week before the school year starts, and ends by mid-June. Having witnessed many seasons that mark time for the student and family, I appreciate that in some years, growth and change is more evident than in other years. The following are details of the scheduled events that host families mark on their calendars.

Within two weeks of welcoming the students, I would hold an orientation and barbecue. I usually scheduled it the last Sunday in August, because many families choose the Labor Day weekend to travel. Since this gathering included the foreign exchange students and their host families, a large home and yard were necessary. Phil and I would provide hamburgers, hot dogs, and cold drinks, and each family would bring side dishes to share. The group numbered about fifty people. Fortunately, there was always one family with a spacious yard who would volunteer to host the event. Sometimes there was a swimming pool or an area to set up a volleyball net. Both of these activities were excellent icebreakers. A family who lives in a community where there is a clubhouse was another option.

During the orientation, the code of conduct, signed by the students in their home country, was reread and signed again. This describes what the student can and cannot do during their stay. They are not allowed to drink, use drugs, drive, or break any of our government's laws or their school or host family's rules.

Although exchange students aren't allowed to drive, many get a learner's permit and some a license. Requirements differ from state to state. Since Colorado requires fifty hours of driving experience for teenagers before they can take the test, it is almost impossible for exchange students to get a license. Nevertheless, a certain number achieve this goal. Students can apply for an international license and drive at sixteen if they can pass the test. Getting a license is especially attractive for German students, since in Germany it costs several thousand dollars, and the minimum driving age is eighteen. Host families are discouraged from allowing exchange students to use their car, however, because if there is an accident their insurance may not cover the cost.

Another important subject is money. It is important for students to understand that none of the money the parents have paid for the program goes to the host family. Students and families are not to borrow money from one another, and the exchange students are advised not to take much money to school. There is also a discussion about who pays. The natural parents are required to provide their children with approximately $200 per month to cover the cost of school supplies, school fees, clothes, toiletry items, and entertainment. The host family's responsibility is to provide lodging and meals. Sometimes the family offers to pay for their exchange student when they go to a movie or do something special, although it isn't a requirement.

A chart showing the chain of contact is reviewed at the orientation. Students are encouraged to discuss problems with their host family before they contact their natural parents. The parents are helpless to do anything, and it creates anxiety. If, after they speak with their hosts, they still have concerns, they are to call their AR. If for some reason the AR can't resolve the issue, they have the regional manager or regional director to call for support. The national office is contacted in extreme situations. One of the staff members calls or e-mails the sending partner, who alerts the natural parents. Most issues never go past the AR. Today, with cell phones and Skype, students are in contact with their natural parents often.

At the orientation, we would talk about school at length. If the students are seniors, they are not allowed to pressure the school for a diploma. The schools I worked with sometimes issued a certificate of attendance but not an actual diploma. By the time of the orientation, students have registered for classes, and many questions have been answered.

During the first student event, all the Germans, all the Asians, and all Spanish speakers pair off and sit together in small groups. Frequently the Brazilians, who are Portuguese-speaking, join the Spanish-speaking students.

The Brazilians can understand Spanish, though the Spanish speakers can't understand Portuguese. It always amazes me how quickly they find each other and start speaking their native language. A roster with the names, street addresses, phone numbers, school, and country of origin for each exchange student and family is distributed at the orientation. This enables host families to carpool for future events and allows exchange students to contact one another. They are encouraged to make American friends, although sometimes it is comforting for them to talk to someone who speaks their native language. Their most difficult challenge, in fact, is to make American friends. American students are initially friendly, but it takes a while for them to include the exchange students in their circle of friends.

The next time we would get together was in October. For eight years, from 1996–2003, I arranged a fall weekend trip to the Y-Camp at Estes Park for the entire region. By August, when I knew how many exchange students had been placed in the metro Denver area, I set the date, reserved the cabins, ordered box lunches, recruited drivers and chaperones, notified students of their carpools, assigned roommates, sent lists of required items, arranged activities, collected the money, and applied to the park for passes.

The students, area representatives, and parents—acting as chaperones and providing transportation—headed for the mountains in autumn. We left Denver on Saturday morning with full cars, skirting Boulder, going through the town of Lyons, and then winding through the Big Thompson Canyon. Our goal was to meet at McDonald's in Estes Park by noon. We descended upon the fast food chain like a swarm of locusts. Many of the students were meeting each other for the first time. All the teenagers were familiar with McDonald's and loved the hamburgers and fries.

After lunch, the group spent about an hour walking through the touristy town, a short distance from the east entrance of Rocky Mountain National Park. After strolling through town, everyone returned to the McDonald's parking lot, and we drove to the camp for the 2:00 p.m. check-in. Although the YMCA of the Rockies isn't far from town, it seems worlds apart from the busy, congested village. Sprawling over hundreds of acres are cabins, skating rinks, swimming pools, basketball courts, a dining hall, horse stables, and a miniature golf course.

Checking in at the main desk, I collected the room keys and attempted to distribute them, along with room assignments and dining hall cards. Following check-in, the students were free until dinner. They could participate in any of the available camp activities. A pick-up volleyball game in front of the lodge was popular. Hiking, arts and crafts, miniature golf, and skating were other options.

A few times, with the help of the camp activities director, a scavenger hunt was planned for late afternoon. Students were divided into teams and given a list of items to find, such as a pine cone, aspen leaf, horseshoe, or miniature golf tee. It was an icebreaker, forcing the members of the team to cooperate and get to know one another.

We all met for dinner at six o'clock p.m. in front of the large dining hall. Our group was not the only one at the camp, so when we entered the dining room, we shared the space with hundreds of others. Standing in long lines didn't bother the teens: they had more time to talk. Following dinner was a planned activity that changed from year to year. The first fall, a campfire sing-along and marshmallow roast seemed like a good idea. It was a flop. Our popular American camp songs were unfamiliar to the exchange students. The leader passed out sheets of music, but it was dark, and no one could read the words. It was also too cold to be outdoors for any length of time in the mountains at night when the temperatures drop dramatically.

For a few years, a dance instructor was hired to teach the group square dancing. That was a hit. With few exceptions, everyone participated. It was a nonverbal activity, and they were all beginners. Several seasons later, when the dance teacher was no longer available, the students were given choices. One group went skating, another swimming, and a third played basketball. An AR supervised each of the activities, which were in different buildings.

By 10:00 p.m., following a snack, the chaperones attempted to lead all the students back to their dorm-style cabins. The sleeping quarters were approximately a ten-minute walk across the campgrounds. By 11:00 p.m. everyone was in his or her bunk, with the lights out, but rarely asleep. Alarms went off at 7:00 a.m. Mornings were crisp, with a light frost on the windows and grass, so getting the teens up, out of bed, and to the dining hall for breakfast took some coaxing.

After a full, American-style breakfast, everyone picked up a preordered box lunch and returned to her cabin. While students and chaperones were packing and loading, the cars lined up outside the main lodge. I was returning keys and settling the bill. When everyone was accounted for we caravanned the half-hour ride into Rocky Mountain National Park.

The three-mile round-trip hike was considered easy. Before starting the hike, the leaders staggered the group so that forty noisy teenagers wouldn't overwhelm the other hikers or animals. A few leaders backed up the last hikers. If there was any grumbling or complaining, it was from those who had stayed up most of the night talking. Occasionally a teen who had never taken a hike before questioned what we were doing besides walking. Observing nature in a spectacular setting, while walking, is an unfamiliar concept to some teens. This isn't cultural, but typical of the age. It might just as easily have been a comment made by a teenager from New York City as from Rome.

Most of the hike was spent taking pictures. Just about every exchange student has a camera. When the group climbed up on a massive boulder or came to a panoramic vista, a dozen cameras sailed back and forth between owner and photographer. Sometimes half a dozen cameras hung around the neck of the one snapping pictures.

The final part of the trail narrowed into a rocky, somewhat steep incline, requiring the hikers to proceed single file. After we scrambled to the top of the rise, the trail opened up to our first glimpse of Emerald Lake, a true gem. Regardless of nationality, teenagers are far less impressed by scenery and more concerned about their stomachs, so they were happy when we stopped for lunch. Contentedly relaxing and enjoying lunch in this tranquil setting didn't last long, however. Gray jays, affectionately known as camp robbers, perched attentively in nearby pines. Suddenly, in one continuous motion, a jay would swoop down, scooping up anything edible. Every year part of a sandwich was lifted from the hand of an unsuspecting victim. A startled reaction provoked gales of laughter. Another teen was more than willing to share his sandwich. In fact, hands shot up, waving part of a lunch in an attempt to attract another robber while their friend snapped a picture.

The return hike, downhill, went faster. Before the teens returned to their cars, they exchanged phone numbers and hugs. For many it was difficult to say good-bye to their weekend roommate or newfound friend.

Everyone piled into the cars they had come in and traveled the two-plus hours back to Denver and surrounding areas. By the time we passed Estes Park, most of the teens were asleep, sprawled across the back seat. By Sunday evening when everyone was safely home, I experienced relief and exhaustion. Fortunately, no one ever got sick, injured, or lost. For some of the exchange students, it was their first and only experience in the Colorado Rockies.

The group got larger, the arrangements got more complicated, and I got older, so the weekend outings became day trips. For the next several years, instead of going to Estes Park, we hiked on a Saturday morning at a nearby mountain park. Following the hike was a picnic lunch; then the kids enjoyed an afternoon at an indoor facility offering laser tag, miniature golf, skating, game machines, bowling, and noise that was more popular with the teens than the adult chaperones. At the end of the day, we went to an all-you-can-eat buffet.

When environmental concerns became an important issue, "being green" extended to the exchange program. For our Saturday fall event, we began volunteering to harvest part of an eighty-acre pumpkin and gourd patch for the Denver Botanical Gardens. Host parents and siblings were invited to participate. As many hands as possible picked the gourds and pumpkins from the vines and placed them into buckets, which, when full, were dumped into a large box, then emptied onto a pickup truck. Several teens tossed the pumpkins to a few boys who stood on the truck bed, catching and piling them. When the truck was filled, the person in charge drove to another field where the pumpkins were unloaded by other students and later sold to the public.

It was hard work and, as a token of appreciation, the exchange students were given free passes to go through the corn maze when they finished the harvest. Adjacent to the arboretum is an eight-acre maze with 2,400 rows of corn standing eight feet high. One of the most frequented mazes in the country, this is yet another fundraiser for the Gardens. By the time the students successfully navigated the labyrinth, it was lunchtime. Host families and ARs drove the students a few miles to a leisurely lunch. The event ended by early afternoon.

In December a holiday-Christmas party was held on a Saturday or Sunday afternoon. In the early nineties, the group was small enough that the party was held in private homes. One Christmas, when an AR was entertaining the small group at her townhouse, she invited me to drop by to see her tree, play some games, and greet her students. When I arrived, several games were in progress. Four kids were playing Scrabble. Since I am an aficionado of the game, always hoping to learn some new words, I pulled up a chair to watch. Somewhat confused, I discovered that I didn't know any of the words. Then I realized that the players were taking turns randomly placing tiles on the board to form words in their native language. Each of the four students spoke a different language. It took will power to squelch my impulse to explain the rules and teach them to play the game properly and in English. Realizing that they were having a congenial, enjoyable time, and playing the game according to the rules was unimportant, I kept quiet, never ceasing to be impressed with foreign students' creativity, ingenuity, and adaptability.

As the student numbers increased and houses were too small, it became necessary to rent a room in a church, which we did for several years. If a host family lived in a community with a clubhouse, the party room was often available. This worked for several more years. We had outgrown private homes when we discovered Amy's.

Built in the 1890s, Amy's, a private Victorian home, was the perfect venue. The first floor is used as a restaurant that serves Sunday brunch and daily lunches. After many years, a large, attractive party room with wood floors, a grand piano, and enough tables for ample seating was added. It became the location for our holiday party. It was cozy and festive, with a Christmas tree and decorations. The bedrooms are on the second and third floors. Monica, the owner, hosted a female student every year. From time to time, students helped serve Sunday brunch. This was an opportunity for them to earn some extra money and the guests enjoyed conversing with the girls.

Since this event was for the entire region, about fifty students attended, including host siblings. The area representatives provided most of the food and beverages. Monica contributed a few of her specialties. In December the weather was generally cold, often with blowing snow and icy roads; it was a popular event, however, and all the exchange students tried to be there. Frequently host brothers and sisters did the driving.

Students were asked to bring a $10 wrapped gift, suitable for a boy or girl. It was a Chinese auction exchange, so no one knew who would wind up with which present. Every participant pulled a number from a bag. The student with number one could choose any gift in the pile and open it. The next teen could choose any unopened package or take the opened one. If the person's gift was taken, they could then select another from the pile or from another student. Each gift could be traded no more than three times. Taking another person's gift was a strange concept to the exchange students. Considering it rude to take something from someone else, they usually kept what they opened. It was difficult to change this way of thinking until the American host brothers and sisters, who had no problem "stealing," demonstrated how it worked. After that, almost apologetically they would take something they really wanted from another person.

Every year there was one gift that was the most coveted. Early on, the teens were unsophisticated. One Christmas, a small stuffed teddy bear dressed in a Broncos shirt was the prize. Another time a Nerf football was traded the customary three times; then the proud owner and the rest of the group went outdoors and played touch football. As the years passed, gift certificates were in vogue. One year the sought-after certificate was Blockbusters, another time, Chipotle. When Starbucks became popular with high school students, those certificates were treasured. Candy is always popular.

The required midyear orientation took place in January or February at one of the host family homes. It was the halfway point in the school year, a time to evaluate the first semester and set realistic expectations and goals for the second. If students were having any problems with their families, sometimes they felt comfortable sharing their concern with other students. It was also an opportunity for the students who arrived for the second semester to integrate into the group.

My favorite activity of the midyear meeting was when the students were asked to draw two simple stick figures. At the top of one of the pages of the orientation packet was the question WHO AM I! Below were two boxes. In the first box the students were asked to draw themselves when they first arrived. In the next box they were to draw themselves five months later. Both pictures were drawn at the midyear meeting. Besides the obvious physical changes—hair longer, girls fatter, boys taller and more muscular—a frequent illustration was the student alone with her suitcases when she arrived; five months later, many of them showed themselves surrounded by friends or at least holding hands with one friend. In the first picture, depicting when they arrived, they drew downturn frowns, but by second semester they drew smiley faces. One of the best illustrations was a drawing of a boy frowning, saying, "Oh! I don't know English and American culture." The second picture showed a figure with a huge smile and kicking up his heels saying, "Yahoo! I know English and a lot of American friends." Realizing how much their English has improved and how their confidence has grown puts a smile on my face. Stressing their accomplishments encourages them to continue improving.

Following the orientation was a potluck prepared by the exchange students. Everyone was asked to bring a dish from her home country to share. Even the boys who claimed they didn't know how to cook managed to create something they were proud to contribute. Examples of a representative meal were cinnamon rolls, egg rolls, fried rice, noodles with beef, pasta, potato pancakes, apple sauce, German potato salad, sausage and sauerkraut, succulent sweet pork, fish cakes, chicken, chocolate cake, and crepes with Nutella, a chocolate hazelnut mixture. Everything was tasty and surprisingly well prepared, but not once did a student bring anything green like a salad or vegetable. A glance across the table revealed a monochromatic color scheme ranging in shades from creamy beige to dark brown. Lack of some green, growing thing didn't seem like a problem to the students, who enjoyed sampling each other's dishes and the party atmosphere. Not only were they becoming familiar with American culture, the exchange students represented so many different countries, they were learning about each other as well.

One of the most universal foods is pizza. In March, families and students met for an early Sunday dinner of pizza and salad. It was not a required event, but was another opportunity for the students to get together, this time with their host family. It also provided a chance for the AR to make sure that students and families weren't experiencing any problems. Sometimes I would host the group while other years we met in a restaurant like Beau Jo's. Pizza was popular with all the students no matter where they were from: the Brazilians preferred ham and pineapple toppings; the German girls liked vegetarian; and almost everyone loved pepperoni.

April is the beginning of baseball season. A Sunday afternoon home Rockies game was a yearly event since baseball is such a part of American culture. Approximately one hundred tickets were purchased for host families, students, and friends. Because the tickets were inexpensive, the seats were high up in the stands, with a bird's-eye view for watching the plays. Truth be known, very few students actually watched the game. They enjoyed eating hot dogs and peanuts and the seventh-inning stretch, when they sang "Take me out to the ballgame"; it was another opportunity to get together. Baseball can be slow-moving, and teenagers enjoy more action. Nevertheless, all the tickets were sold every spring.

The final activity was the required reentry orientation. By May, getting everyone together on any given day was burdensome. Weekends were impossible. Between proms, graduations, finals, and parties, a weekday evening was the best chance for perfect attendance. Some years, the orientation for students was followed by an ice cream social where everyone made their own sundae with all the trimmings. Other years, a barbecue and potluck dinner, including the host families, was a pleasant way to end the year.

It was rewarding to see how these young people had become more confident, mature, independent, and comfortable. Now there were no boundaries with language. All the students were dreaming and speaking in English. They no longer broke off into their little ethnic groups but instead intermingled.

The reentry orientation helped exchange students prepare to leave their host families and the new friends they had made. When they left their home countries, they knew they would be returning in five or ten months. They didn't know when they would get back to the United States. The orientation also helped them realize that they might experience reverse cultural shock when they got home. Certain behaviors that they had grown up with might now seem annoying. Families and friends would expect them to be the same, not realizing how much they had changed. Besides physical changes, they had become more independent. It was important for them to understand that they would probably want to talk about their experience far more than their friends would be interested in listening. Students who didn't think they would have any problems e-mailed months later to say that it was more of an adjustment than they had anticipated.

A certain number of students didn't want to leave. Most of them had mixed emotions. I suggested leaving notes if they couldn't bring themselves to say good-bye. Mainly, I encouraged them to invite their host families to visit them in their home country or talk about when they would come back to Colorado. Some families tearfully expressed that they had no idea how difficult it would be to take their student to the airport and say good-bye.

The calendar year ended in June when all the students left. Some years were more successful than others, although every year I thought I had just had the best group ever. Remembering when they arrived, I was always amazed by how grownup and self-assured they had become.

I was usually still placing new students who would be arriving in August. By July, our schools were all on vacation and not accepting any more placements. With the exception of the host family orientation, prior to the students' arrival, there was a brief respite.

Chapter 9

Cultural Differences—The Fruit

The joy of planting a fruit tree occurs when you walk into your garden, pick and take a bite out of that first juicy peach, or have enough apples to bake a pie. Equally rewarding is the shade provided on a hot, summer day when you feel cooled by a canopy of dense leaves from a maple, ash, or oak tree.

Some of the best benefits of welcoming an exchange student into your home come from the conversations that happen while you are sitting around your kitchen table. Like the tree that continues to produce, season after season, once you become aware and open to cultural differences, the knowledge is yours forever and the process continues toward greater understanding. Exchange students want to learn about America, but they also want to share information about their culture. Take advantage of every opportunity to learn from your new family member. Frequently they bring a book about their country and are disappointed when their host family displays it on the coffee table and rarely opens it or doesn't ask their student to talk about where and how they live. As well as becoming part of a family and adjusting to school, international students experience differences in languages, customs, religious beliefs, greetings, personal space, bathroom etiquette, food, and values.

Language

One Sunday afternoon, while I was walking through Cherry Creek mall with Fabio, he casually asked a question. He had been an exchange student for several months. His English was good. He wanted to know, "What's *stuff*?" We had been window-shopping, following lunch, when he posed the question. I gave a quick answer by pointing to a crowded window and saying, "See all those things? That's stuff." He seemed satisfied with my explanation and we continued our outing. I wasn't satisfied with my answer, however. Later on, I looked for the meaning of "stuff." There are pages of definitions and examples. *To stuff candy in your pocket; to stuff a turkey; a pillow stuffed with feathers; the trunk was full of stuff; my nose is stuffed; wheat is the stuff they use to make bread; put your stuff away; get rid of all that stuff; I ate too much, I'm stuffed; he's a stuffed shirt; worthless or foolish ideas in speech or writing—stuff and nonsense; informal drink or drugs; things in which one is knowledgeable—knows his stuff; in baseball, a pitcher's ability to produce such spin or control the speed of a pitch; an expression of contempt—stuff it.* English is confusing. No wonder Fabio had asked the question. Increasingly, I am impressed with foreigners' ability to learn and understand all the idioms and nuances our language presents. It is also interesting to observe how often Americans use the word *stuff* in their daily conversation.

Several times students were embarrassed when they used an incorrect word or a word that changed the meaning. A German girl blushed when she described how the students in her class laughed when she asked to borrow a rubber. She didn't realize that American students use the word *eraser* and that the word *rubber* has a sexual connotation. In another instance, when Jonas from Sweden went to a Chinese restaurant with his host family for the first time, he looked at the menu and exclaimed, "Human beef" instead of "Hunan beef." The family chuckled and explained his mistake. American students have trouble pronouncing some foreign names. Yan smiled when she talked about her name. One classmate said, "Your name is easy to say. I won't have a problem. It is like Japanese money," and he called her Yen. Another person thought it sounded like our word for sweet potato and called her Yam.

Reading the students' letters was helpful. I got insights not revealed in their bios. They often describe their interests, expectations, and responsibilities. It also enabled me to evaluate their written English. When students described their chores, they wrote about "hoovering." Hoover vacuums were so popular in the United Kingdom during the twentieth century that *Hoover* became a verb. Even though Hoover vacuums are no longer popular today, Europeans still say they are "hoovering " when referring to vacuuming.

Customs

I took a short hike one autumn Saturday morning with Luisa, a Brazilian. The popular trail was a narrow one in the foothills. It was sunny and unseasonably warm, and dozens of people had the same idea. As we passed other hikers, we greeted one another with "Hello" or "Good morning." When we finished our hike an hour later, Luisa commented that I sure knew a lot of people. She thought that the people with whom I had exchanged greetings were friends of mine. I told her that I didn't know any of these people, but saying hello is the courteous, customary thing to do. Luisa explained that no one in Brazil would say hello to a complete stranger, even though Brazilians are warm and friendly to people they know. She then went on to say that the kids at school ask, "How are you doing?" but before she can answer, they are on to something else. She was disheartened to realize that they didn't really want to know about her. Asking how you are is just a greeting. This led Luisa and other students to describe Americans as being superficial. It was a cultural difference that disappointed them. They felt that friendships among US teens were shallower than their relationships. On the other hand, exchange students repeatedly describe Americans as friendly—friendlier than the people from their own countries—and they like that quality.

Bathroom Etiquette

Eduardo, from Brazil, received the highest praise from his host family whenever the AR checked on his progress. He was polite, smart, and eager to please. Every month when the AR called the host family, they would report that everything was going quite well. During one call they said there was an issue. At first, they were too embarrassed to mention it, but finally their frustration hit a peak. Eduardo would not put the toilet paper in the toilet. The family had talked to Eduardo; he continued putting the paper in a wastebasket however, because this was what he did at home. It was difficult for him to break the habit. Feeling uncomfortable discussing this delicate subject, the host family didn't mention it again to Eduardo but told the AR. The area representative suggested mentioning it to him again, and a second discussion solved the problem.

I had little patience when I was told about this situation. It seemed like a pretty simple request.

The following year our exchange program conference was in Brazil. Except at luxurious hotels designed for tourists, no one put the paper in the toilet. Brazil's plumbing system can't handle it. Everywhere I went, a wastebasket was used for disposal. Frequently, as the toilet paper was dropping irretrievably out of my hand into the toilet, I would think to myself, "Oh no! What's the matter with me? I did it again." In situations like this, we don't think but rather follow a habit that has been ingrained in us from childhood. Bettina Hansel, in her book *The Exchange Student Survival Kit*, refers to this as "deep culture." Daily patterns that are automatic and not thought about are difficult to change. I finally had more appreciation for Eduardo's dilemma. In *Host Family Survival Kit,* Nancy King and Ken Huff describe "deep culture as out-of-awareness 'cultural baggage' that exchange students bring with them or, more accurately, with themselves." Americans carry cultural baggage too.

Another student also had a bathroom issue. A German sending partner shared the following story at a meeting. It had been told to her after the student returned to Germany. Helga wouldn't close the door when she used the toilet. Her host family thought this was a cultural difference and didn't mention it at first; then it started to bother them. When they asked her why she didn't close the door so that she would have some privacy, she responded that she would really like to, but the bathroom didn't have a door. Helga didn't realize that there was a pocket door—something not used in Germany. The family never thought to explain this. Of course, the student never thought to ask. Evidently she didn't see other family members closing the door.

Names

I made several observations about names that piqued my curiosity enough to learn their origins. One's name is an important aspect of one's identity. In addition to mispronouncing them, Americans seldom understand the origin or the order of names. If their name was an especially difficult one, the students gave themselves a nickname, rather than listen to their name being mispronounced all year. China, Vietnam, Korea, and Japan place the surname first, then the middle name, and finally the given name. For example, if the name is Anh Tu Nguyen it is written Nguyen Tu Anh. Japanese don't have middle names. Hungarians also put the surname first, then the given name.

After years of supervising Vietnamese exchange students, I noticed that a good percentage had the last name Nguyen. It is the most common family name in Vietnam, claimed by 40 percent of the people. It is pronounced Win. Although not all Vietnamese who have this name can trace their heritage back to China, Nguyen is a Chinese name.

Spanish families give their children several middle names, frequently after saints. Spain and Mexico use the following order: given name, middle names, father's name, then mother's maiden name. A Mexican girl might be called Maria Luisa Catherina Garcia Valdez or a Spanish boy Miguel San Roman Delgado. Brazilians reverse the parents' names. After the given names is the mother's maiden name, then the father's family name.

Russian names are given gender endings. Boys' names typically end in the suffix *ov, in,* or *ev* and girls would be *ova, ina,* or *eva.* The endings *ovich* or *ovna* are also commonly used. Children are named for their fathers and have a patronymic or middle name. All surnames from the Czech Republic end in *ov* for the masculine or *ova* for the feminine.

The exchange students who come from Thailand have long surnames with between twelve and fourteen letters that are difficult for Americans to pronounce. Native Thai family names are short. If the name was long, it was an indication that their families left China during the Cultural Revolution. After they settled in Thailand, they applied to the government for a new name that was unique. If two people have the same surname they are related because otherwise everyone has a different name. The names kept getting longer so there was less chance of duplication. Every family submitted five names to the government, hoping that at least one would be original. First names are a little shorter, but not any easier to pronounce. Examples are Phachara and Nuttawat. Before they come to the United States, Thai students pick American names that don't seem to relate to their given names but are easy to pronounce. For instance, there was a Nan, a Bright, and a Dada.

German surnames are frequently occupational. Every village had similar trades from which the people took their names, so people of different German villages who had the same trade and therefore the same surname were not necessarily related to each other. Some Germans who have immigrated to the United States have changed the spelling of their name. For example; Meyer, Mayer,

Maier, and Meier all have the same meaning: a tenant farmer. Some common German surnames are derived from locations, such as berg (mountain), burg (castle), holz (woods).

Religion

Buddhist, Christian, Jewish, Hindu, and Muslim exchange students represent all the major religions. A good percentage of the applicants in our program are Catholic, coming from Central and South America, France, Italy, Poland, Spain, and southern Germany. The rest of Germany is predominantly Protestant. The Asians represented are Buddhist and Christian. South Koreans are for the most part Christian, occasionally Catholic. Only a few Jewish applicants apply each year; they usually prefer placements with Jewish families. Some keep kosher, and that creates an additional challenge in finding a family. The Islamic students are generally nonpracticing, but none of them eat pork because of tradition. Russians, Central Asians, Chinese, and Eastern Europeans frequently list no religion.

Regardless of the students' religion, they practice it differently in their home country. If the family wants the exchange student to attend church, the student usually cooperates. I emphasized at the orientations that families might request—but can't require—that their exchange students attend services. Even if they don't want to go to the religious service, teens enjoy youth group, which offers another opportunity to make American friends.

There are three questions about religion on the application. The student is asked her religious preference, how frequently she attends church in the home country and whether she would be willing to attend with her host family if the religion is different from her own. Students have shared with their host families that during the interview in their home country they are coached to indicate some religious participation. Other countries view Americans as churchgoers. The partners fear that if a student indicates no religious preference or unwillingness to attend with the host family, they will have a more difficult time being placed.

Religion played a significant role for Bruna, a short, squat Bolivian girl with Indian features who had a strict Catholic upbringing. She spent her exchange year with a Mormon family. Bruna was eighteen and had graduated from high school when she arrived. I didn't know that when I placed her. The schools I worked with frowned upon graduates. After being chastised for the omission on her application, she was genuinely remorseful and apologized. In all other respects, Bruna was a compliant, obedient girl. Every school assignment was carefully completed and on time, which contributed to her 4.0 grade-point average. Her host family commented that she followed all the rules of their household and was always anxious to please. In the spring, Bruna began expressing a desire to return to the United States to go to college; after her year here, she returned to Bolivia according to program rules.

Unable to support her dream financially or philosophically, Bruna's parents expected that she would attend a public university in Bolivia and live at home. Her host family was in a position to help her and offered to sponsor her education. That fall Bruna enrolled at a Mormon college in Utah where her host brother was a junior and the younger host sister would attend the following year. During her sophomore year she met a young man whom she married after graduation.

Although Bruna had been raised as an observant Catholic, she joined the Church of Jesus Christ of Latter-day Saints and was married in the home of her host family. I sent a gift, and we got together once after the wedding when she was visiting her host family. Bruna told me that she was happy in her marriage and her religion and about living in Utah, but her Bolivian parents were very sad. They hadn't come to the wedding and didn't understand their daughter's choices.

Personal Space and Greetings

Various cultures have different comfort levels about personal space. Americans generally stand an average of thirty inches apart from each other and stand in the same place during a conversation. Many Southern Europeans have an intimate distance of only eight to eleven inches. Japanese are comfortable standing ten inches apart. Asians are used to a closer personal space because of their crowded cities. Sensitivity to these cultural differences helps to make the foreign exchange student comfortable.

Traveling to Kyoto on a bullet train called *Shinkansen*, I observed a passing commuter train headed for Tokyo during morning rush hour. The passengers standing by the doors were so crammed that their faces were flattened against the windows. That image has stayed with me. At their most crowded times, American subways and buses have ample space by comparison. I have been on New York City subways at busy times and didn't experience what I witnessed in Japan.

Twenty years ago, my own cultural awareness regarding personal space was heightened while visiting Greece. My son and I were on the island of Santorini, sitting on a bench waiting for a bus. By American standards, this bench was designed for two people. We both could be described as slender, but the bench was still only comfortable for a duo. Along came a stocky, burly, native with a head of thick, dark hair, smoking a cigarette. He wedged himself between us, creating an uncomfortable situation. His muscular leg pressed against my left thigh while his arm rested against mine. David was experiencing close contact on his right side. Without saying a word, David and I stood up at exactly the same time, leaving the confused Greek sitting alone. We thought he was rude.

Over the next several days, I noticed that Greeks had a different comfort level when it comes to personal space. They sit closer to one another than Americans, even if they are strangers. It is not uncommon for natives to sit with their backs touching or friends facing one another with not much more than a nose-length distance between them. They are "in your face," but not in an aggressive way.

Later that week, while sitting on a bar stool at a small stand eating a gyro, a local sitting behind me, eating his sandwich, casually brushed his back against mine. This time the close proximity didn't bother me. I was able to continue eating my lunch without feeling uncomfortable. Although I felt the slight pressure from his back, I had already accepted it as part of the Greek culture. Reflecting back a few days, I realized that we were the ones with the questionable manners when we got up from the bench.

A culture gram describing customs of their student's country is provided to every host family. At the airport, when families meet their exchange student for the first time, knowing the proper greeting starts things off in a positive way. Greetings differ from culture to culture.

For example, Latin Americans, Italians, Spaniards, and French kiss on each cheek. "Scandinavians are happy with a single kiss, the French mostly prefer a double. Americans are continually confused about greeting kisses and bump noses as they fumble their way through a single peck."[2] Japanese people bow at a first meeting, the person with the highest status bowing the least and the one with the least status bowing the most. Whether or not someone will be offended by being touched during conversation depends on her culture. Along with Americans, Japanese, Germans, and English don't like to be touched. Japanese do not like to have their head touched ever. It is considered disrespectful. Although a few times I observed Japanese girls give a hug to their host mom at first meeting, I suspect that the orientation in Japan discussed American greetings.

Values

Values differ from culture to culture. Honesty ranks high on the list for Americans. We grew up hearing that George Washington could not tell a lie and admitted to cutting down the cherry tree. Parson Weems created this fictional story in the early 1800s for his book, *The Life and Memorable Actions of George Washington.* Nevertheless, it is a story dear to Americans. Another example of the

2.   Allan Pease, Barbara Pease, *The Definitive Book of Body Language,* Bantam Dell, 2004, p. 114.

importance of honesty in the United States is the reference to Abraham Lincoln as "honest Abe." *Truth is virtuous* is an axiom frequently repeated.

Prospective host families are asked to list the rules for their family members. It is not unusual for a parent with children to mention honesty, explaining that their children have been brought up to tell the truth. Host parents stress that lying is unacceptable. They expect their exchange student always to be forthright.

In Asian cultures, avoiding bringing shame to oneself or to one's family is an important value. Lying to save face or to prevent family disgrace is acceptable. "If you say something a Japanese doesn't agree with, he'll still say yes—or *Hai* in Japanese—to keep you talking. A Japanese yes usually means, 'Yes, I heard you' and not 'Yes, I agree.' For example, if you say to a Japanese person, 'You don't agree, do you?' he will nod his head and say yes even though he may not agree."[3] In Latin cultures, lying is permissible if it prevents hurt feelings. When host parents told me that their foreign exchange student had lied to them, and they now felt distrustful, the reason, was often cultural. Understanding why their student felt the need to lie was important.

Kim, a South Korean girl, was spending her last weekend in our home before returning to Seoul. It was a hot June day with temperatures in the nineties. We had been to the zoo in the morning and had stopped for lunch. Kim selected sushi. Unable to finish her lunch, she asked to take the plastic box containing the leftovers with her. When we got home, Kim headed for her room on the lower level. In a few hours, I realized that the raw

3.   Allan Pease, Barbara Pease, *The Definitive Book of Body Language*, Bantam Dell, 2004, p. 117.

fish, sitting down in the bedroom, should be refrigerated. I called down to Kim to bring the sushi upstairs and refrigerate it. She had already eaten it, but for some reason was embarrassed that she had taken it to her bedroom. It was easier for her to tell me the sushi had disappeared. Kim said she didn't know what had happened to the rolls, but they were gone. She was able to produce the empty bag and container. She averted her eyes when I spoke to her. This bothered me, and I thought that she was lying. Finally realizing that she was trying to save face, I dropped the subject.

In the United States, if someone won't maintain eye contact with another person, he or she is not considered trustworthy. Looking directly at the person you are talking to is encouraged. Eye contact means different things in different cultures. "Try not to stare at a Japanese when you talk to him. Many Japanese feel it is rude to look a person directly in the face; 'if the person has an ugly face he will feel uncomfortable'—this is the way it was once explained. The Japanese are very considerate not to hurt other people's feelings," according to Samuel E. Martin in his book, *Easy Japanese*.[4]

---

4.   Samuel E. Martin, *Easy Japanese*, Charles E. Tuttle, 1998, p. 4.

Food

If not the most basic, food is certainly an important aspect of most cultures. What we eat is ingrained in us from childhood. Exchange students have a difficult time adjusting not only to what we eat, but how and when. Surprisingly, midway through the year nearly all of them love Chipotle and Chili's.

Americans can relate to the smell of bacon and eggs cooking first thing in the morning; in their native country, Asians wake up to the smell of fried rice. Cooking rice for breakfast is customary. Some Asians eat it three times a day. The family who was hosting Melee, from Japan, became accustomed to her cooking rice, but they would only buy brown rice. Melee's host family, along with millions of other Americans, are eating healthfully and believe that brown rice is healthier since it hasn't had the nutrients removed by processing. White rice is what Asians have eaten since they were babies, and many of them don't like brown rice. According to the World Health Organization (WHO), Japanese have the longest healthy life expectancy in the world.

Throughout Central and South America, rice and beans make up the basic diet. The natives eat it for breakfast, lunch, and dinner. During a trip to Costa Rica, for every meal I had a choice between pinto *gallo* or *gallo* pinto (beans and rice or rice and beans).

In an invitation to the host family International potluck dinner, I asked each family to bring a dish representing their student's country. Sometimes the families who had been corresponding with their students asked for a family recipe. Others went online or read cookbooks. Examples of exotic dishes included Vietnamese spring rolls, paella, rice and beans, quiche, *feijoadas*, sausage and kraut, enchiladas, Pad Thai, strudel, and German chocolate cake. Never suggesting what anyone should bring, I was always surprised with the excellent variety. One year, however, when I had placed more than the usual number of German students, almost everyone brought a dish containing potatoes. There was potato salad, German potato salad, potato pancakes, potato dumplings, kraut, sausage, and potatoes. A family hosting a Spanish student brought a Spanish tortilla, similar to a frittata, that is made with potatoes and eggs. After that, I tried to get an idea of what people were planning to prepare and contribute to the dinner.

Not only is the cuisine unique to each country, but also the utensils. Not all Asian countries use chopsticks. Thais use a fork in their left hand and a spoon in the right. This was demonstrated when I took two Thai girls to a Thai restaurant for lunch.

Because of the American diet, most female students gain weight during their stay. I referred to it as the "ten plus pounds." For some reason, boys aren't as likely to gain. Snacking is not popular in other countries the way it is in the United States. Girls seem to eat more and exercise less during their exchange experience. Interestingly, they lose the weight shortly after they return to their home countries. I happened to be in Paris five months after Nicole had finished her year in Colorado. She had been one of the "ten plus pounders," but when I met her, she had returned to her svelte self. French sauces and desserts are rich and fattening, but their portions are smaller, and they don't have seconds. The French walk everywhere, and they don't snack between meals.

When other girls came back to visit their host families a year or two later, every one of them had lost any weight they gained. Before some of the female students arrived, they heard about "getting fat" and ate less than normal during their home stay.

Eva, from Germany, was having problems with her host family. They thought that Eva had an eating disorder, possibly anorexia. She was dropping weight rapidly and refusing to eat what the host dad was preparing. Finally, her natural parents, concerned that the host family was too controlling, asked to have Eva removed from the home. Two weeks before she was to return to Germany she came to live with us.

I knew that Eva preferred not to eat meat, although her application didn't indicate that she was a vegetarian. Carefully, I placed small portions of vegetables, salad, and a starch on her plate. I never made a comment, whether she ate the food or not. As she became more comfortable in our home, she started eating more and looking healthier. By the end of two weeks, we had developed a bond. She has kept in frequent contact after returning to Germany. When she graduated high school two years later, she asked her natural parents for a ticket to come back and visit. Eva had put back all of the weight she had lost and was radiant and happy. We delighted in spending time with her again. We are still in touch. Eva and her parents send us chocolates at Christmastime, and we are kept informed about her advanced education.

Over the years, I have observed that in spite of the differences in language, religion, customs, values, and food, teenagers have more in common than one might expect. The similarities among teens from Europe, North and South America, and the industrialized nations of Asia are greater than the differences. According to a global study of middle-class teenager's rooms in twenty-five industrialized countries indicated it was difficult, if not impossible, to tell whether the rooms were in Los Angeles, Mexico City, Tokyo, Rio de Janeiro, Sydney, or Paris. They dress in Levis and T-shirts and wear Nike shoes. Teenagers listen to the same kinds of music. A top priority is going to a local coffeehouse or wherever the "in" place is at the time and "hanging out" with friends. Talking on their cell phones, text messaging, listening to music, and using the computer occupy a major part of a teenager's day. Acceptance among their peers and making friends are universally important.

Afterword

After this year, I will no longer be managing the program. Area representatives will apply to schools and place students with host families, so that in August new groups will arrive, orientations will be conducted, events planned. The cycle repeats itself. I hope the program will continue to expand and grow so that more families and students have the opportunity to learn from each other about cultural differences that eventually break down barriers, contributing to global understanding. It is impossible for me to measure how much I have learned from twenty-plus years of experience in cultural exchange. I do know that my deepening appreciation for cultural exchange and cultural diversity has become an integral part of who I am, changing forever my sensitivity, knowledge, and awareness of customs, values, and ideas different from my own.

I wish I could say that after one reads *Living with Your Exchange Student*, the world will be a more peaceful place, but I can't. With increased responsiveness and awareness of the importance of diversity, however, small steps are being taken toward this desired goal.

None of us would want to imagine a world without trees. Not only do they provide oxygen that is life-sustaining, but also food, shelter, and beauty. Living in a world void of cultural diversity would be as bleak as a world without trees. For survival and world peace, people must learn to understand one another and embrace the differences. In our "shrinking world," there has never been a more important time to cultivate understanding of other cultures.

I have presented many examples of how families hosting foreign exchange students contribute, albeit slowly, to improving the chances for peaceful relations and the betterment of our planet. Every exchange student who has a positive experience returns to his native country changed forever. He or she no longer has the stereotypical, often negative, view of Americans portrayed on television or in the movies. Bonding with an American family provides opportunities for open communication and mutual respect. It is my hope that after reading *Living with Your Exchange Student* you will be motivated to consider hosting an exchange student or becoming an exchange student or an area representative.

Glossary

apostille: An embossed raised seal legalizing documents for international use. It is in compliance with the provisions of the Hague Convention.

berg: The word for *mountain* in German.

bok choy: Chinese cabbage.

Bouvier des Flandres: A giant breed of dog originating in Flandres.

capoeira: An African-Brazilian art form that combines martial arts, dance, and music. It was performed by the slaves and is still popular today.

daikon: A large, slender, white root similar to a radish.

feijoades: National dish of Brazil made with beans, beef, pork, and vegetables.

gaighoi: An Asian vegetable.

geisha: Japanese women trained to entertain men in the art of tea serving, conversation, music, and dance.

Gion: District in Kyoto, Japan, where kabuki originated in the 1500s.

hajimemash'te: "How are you?" in Japanese.

hijab: Headdress worn by some Muslim women.

holz: German word for *woods.*

kabuki: A form of traditional Japanese drama using song, dance, and mime.

kaiseki: A Japanese meal served in assorted bowls and dishes meant to complement the food.

ohayo: "Good morning" in Japanese.

ryocan: Japanese-style inn.

sayonara: "Good-bye" in Japanese.

shinkansen: Japanese bullet train.

shoji: A Japanese paper screen that acts as a room divider.

Ticos: The name Costa Ricans call themselves.

CPSIA information can be obtained at www.ICGtesting.com
Printed in the USA
BVOW020550190112

280853BV00001BA/1/P